People, Events and Governance

People, Events and Governance

Prasanna Kumar Mishra

BLACK EAGLE BOOKS
Dublin, USA | Bhubaneswar, India

Black Eagle Books
USA address:
7464 Wisdom Lane
Dublin, OH 43016

India address:
E/312, Trident Galaxy, Kalinga Nagar,
Bhubaneswar-751003, Odisha, India

E-mail: info@blackeaglebooks.org
Website: www.blackeaglebooks.org

First International Edition Published by
Black Eagle Books, 2023

PEOPLE, EVENTS AND GOVERNANCE
by **Prasanna Kumar Mishra**

Cover & Interior Design: Ezy's Publication

ISBN- 978-1-64560-370-2 (Paperback)

Printed in the United States of America

To
All those who realised they are
citizens, not subjects.

The one who loves all intensely begins perceiving
in all living beings a part of himself.
He becomes a lover of all, a part and parcel of the
Universal Joy.
He flows with the stream of happiness, and is
enriched by each soul.

Yajur Veda

FOREWARD

These short pieces of writing on people, events and governance, due to my ineptitude, would appear disconnected. That makes an explaining necessary. In a sense, the pieces are windows to my belief system and, as such, indeed are connected to one another. I always believe that it is really a kindly world that has been gifted to us by God to live in and we need to reciprocate the Divine gesture by living a life and doing things that measure us up to His expectations. The litmus test is how kindly we have been in our living, in our journey through life, how kind we have been to people who are under our care and how humane we have been even to those who we do not know but have robbed shoulders with.

Justice Felix Frankfurter had served the Supreme Court of the USA from January 30, 1939 to August 28, 1962 and wrote 247 opinions for the Court, wrote 132 concurring opinions and 251 dissents. Widely known for his erudition, he had said "No office in this land is more important than that of being a citizen." I believe in what he said. The small world around me have revealed enough to learn, to react to, to write about, to articulate my views on, to act as a responsible citizen, rise above prejudices, self-interest and timidity and work for a better society and responsible governance.

While our Constitution grants freedom of speech, Freebies have conferred on the recipients the freedom of silence. The beneficiaries have obliged and have made liberal use of silence. A polity that is constitutionally mandated to be Democratic is going silent and this facilitates irresponsible governance. We have been noticing that Legislatures have been having shorter sessions and most of the days they meet; there is more noise and cacophony than informed discussion on important issues. Media seems focused on TRP. Our polity seems to be drifting towards a zone of silence. There is noise, no doubt, and plenty of it, but preponderantly on non-issues. Citizens, therefore, need to step in and speak.

Citizen's voice should sing different tones-- avoiding sensationalism, not being vitriolic. It should make a symphony of reason, without rancor, without fear or favour. Cacophony never enriched the democratic temper; nor did silence do justice to democracy.

Ruler must have to be reminded again and again about its role. "How should a king behave?" Yudhistira had asked Bhisma." Righteousness", Bhisma had answered," is the watch word of a king. Nothing is greater than that in this world. Malice should have no place in the heart of a king. His senses should be perfectly under control. He should use his intelligence and he will then be glorious: swelling in greatness like the ocean fed with the waters of a thousand rivers." "Poison kills but one man: so does a weapon. But wicked counsels destroy an entire kingdom with kings and subjects."

While health of democracy gets affected due to increasing deficiencies in institutions established primarily to ensure its health, thousand flowers blooming through citizens' voice, might help. This can happen if a concerned and responsible citizenry is on a mission mode, as Martin Luther King Jr said, "Until justice rolls down like water and righteousness like a mighty stream."

I would seek the indulgence of Readers to keep in mind these thoughts of mine.

Basant Panchami, 2023   **Prasanna Kumar Mishra**
Gangotri
BJ-26, Buxi Jagabandhu Nagar
Bhubaneswar- 751014

Contents

The Kindly World

My wife and I had been to Shimla sometime in 2002 summer when Delhi was warm enough and we spent three nights there, in the State Guest House. On the first day, after dinner, my wife suddenly said "I had last seen clouds hitting the hills and rain pouring years ago; how I wish I saw clouds, thunder, lightning and rain in the hills again, during this visit to Shimla" The next morning we visited places in and around Shimla. Chief Secretary, Harsh Gupta, a good friend, had made available a good car and an excellent Driver. While the car was negotiating a climb and the weather was pleasant and sunny, my wife asked the Driver "Do you sometimes get rains in Shimla in this part of the year?" He immediately slowed down the car, craned his neck out of the window, looked up and smilingly said, "No madam, we do not get rains these days; but you should come during the rainy days and see how clouds play with the hills and the bubbling rainwater flow down."

We had a busy day on our second day in Shimla. That night, around eleven, we woke up at the sound of thunder and flashes of lightning. It rained heavily for more than an hour. Perhaps nature conspired to fulfill her wish. She was ecstatic; I found no explanation how it could have happened. We kept watching the rain outside, with awe.

She unfolded yet another wish. She longed to see

a Pahari wedding and wondered if this could take place while we were still at Shimla. She was born in Garhwal but lived mostly in Delhi. During her infrequent visits to the Hills in childhood, she could have seen a few weddings.

We woke up early to the sound of digging of the ground outside. I looked at the garden outside the room. In the front portion of the State Guest House, I saw around fifteen people and a lot of activities. Curious, I went out to find out what exactly was going on. I was told a daughter of a Member of the Himachal Public Service Commission would marry a boy from Gujarat that day and arrangements were being made for the wedding in the State Guest House.

I could not believe that her second wish would also be answered. I rushed to the room to tell her about her second wish materialising. We watched the Pahari wedding as detached onlookers. Our curiosity, however, caught the attention of the bride's father who was happy that my wife's wish was getting fulfilled in his daughter's wedding. We could not decline his warm invitation to stay on for lunch. The sight of ladies carrying water-filled brass pitchers and coming to the marriage pandal was a memorable sight.

We left Shimla happy. I could not be an obstinate rationalist and treat both the experiences as mere coincidence. I would rather gladly acknowledge the pervading presence of a benevolent Higher Force that guides us, protects us and makes us live a happy and contended life. I was convinced that if a wish was said from the heart, the entire universe conspired and helped for the wish to materialise.

❑

Our Avoidable Lifestyle

A voidable lifestyle like sleeping too late and waking up late, indulging in food and drinks, skipping breakfast, liberal recourse to medicines including sleep inducing pills-- even without advice of doctors, love for junk food and tobacco, has been making thousands of young men and women vulnerable to ailments which would have adverse impact on the length and quality of the working life of youths. They know intake of fresh vegetables is desirable, yet they would go for food in restaurants where very often they would settle for spicy and oily dishes. The other day the revelation of an old friend of mine, a widower, was shocking. Housekeeping is with a family that lives in his house and the couple looks after him. The man and wife have a child. Therefore, food is made in the house for four persons. They use at least eight liters of cooking oil per month. My advice to him was to curtail the consumption drastically. "We, five consumers including our support staff, consume 2500 ml of oil per month" I told him. I had to make efforts to make him believe.

Many people in our society love to speak less. They prefer to work and read; they would avoid a crowd or commotion. While this trait need not be decried, I would feel that people should not be averse to engaging themselves in lively and healthy discussions. Quality conversation promotes efficiency of the brain. Positive thinking is a sure way of keeping our brain in shape. By engaging in repartee and keeping our cool, we succeed in keeping away premature wrinkles on the forehead. It adds luster to personality. One looks peaceful rather than ruffled. Decision making ability improves. Probability of wrong decisions is less.

We do not limit our crusade against our natural endowment only to these aberrations I have narrated above. We have gone beyond. How many of us, including the brilliant ones of the emerging generation, get pleasure in writing by hand? Calligraphy used to get reflected many a time in letters written to friends and near and dear ones. Letter writing is on decline. I had great pleasure seeing my grandson writing by hand when he was younger. Now I have started seeing his feelings through e-mails. I only hope he does not abandon writing by hand when he grows up. Regular writing by hand— not limited to putting our signature or writing a cheque -- keeps our reflexes in shape and the fingers agile. Handwriting skill, I believe, reflects the state of health of our brain.

Sadly we seem to be under the impression that the human body is strong enough to withstand relentless abuse. We are wrong. Let us not drift from the normal too radically and too fast. The youths may keep this in mind and ensure that they too enjoy every morning the scene of the sun rising. Let them enjoy the chirping of early morning birds. Bahagvad Gita speaks about SAMATWAM YOGA UCHYATE-- Equanimity is Yoga. A nice example of the precept is the Anantasayanam posture of Lord Vishnu— displaying serenity. Appreciation of this precept would make our young generation aware of the virtue of being in peace with self. It will make them see virtue in moderation. They should appreciate that it may not be wise to tinker too much with the law of nature.

❑

Assembly Sessions Getting Shorter

Explaining what minimum government and maximum governance mean, Prime Minister Narendra Modi in an interview had candidly said that the country is yet to appreciate its real meaning. Giving an example, he had said, "Earlier my Cabinet note would take six months to reach the entire Cabinet. But now it takes only 15 days. This is what minimum government and maximum governance is. Same number of people but the result is more."

With Odisha Assembly sessions getting shorter, it is leading to a public perception that the Temple of Democracy is increasingly losing its shine. The 33-day winter session of Odisha Assembly was scheduled to continue till December 31, 2022. The House, however, functioned for just eight working days. The first Supplementary Budget introduced in the House on November 24 was passed on November 30. The session had many issues to handle including plight of farmers, problems of schoolteachers, black-marketing of fertilizers, etc. Several ministers were away from the Session. The Assembly was adjourned sine die on the first day of December. This is not the first occasion when the session of the Odisha Assembly has been closed much earlier than the scheduled date.

In 2021, Odisha Assembly met for only 43 days. Between 2016 and 2021, the average number of days it met in a year was 42. Odisha has prescribed the minimum number of sitting days at 60. The National Commission to Review the Working of the Constitution (NCRWC) had suggested that state legislatures with less than 70 members should meet for at least 50 days a year, while the rest should meet for at least 90 days. Of course, many state legislatures have been meeting for much lesser days in a year. For example, between 2016 and 2021, 23 state legislatures met for an average of 25 days with Tripura Assembly meeting for 11 days, Punjab, Haryana and Uttarakhand for 14 days and Delhi for 16 days.

Instead of drawing satisfaction for the comparatively higher number of days Odisha legislature has been in session, more important issue is to critically examine if the legislature of a state with over 45 million people with hundreds of important issues ranging from acute poverty to distress induced migration of people, from low agriculture productivity to unsatisfactory harnessing of its abundant water resources, from poor railway network to widespread corruption, should not discharge its constitutional responsibility to ensure high quality governance by the Executive that is mandated to be accountable to it. In 2021, Odisha legislature passed 20 Bills while state legislatures of India passed an average of 21 Bills. The highest number of Bills, 48, was passed by Karnataka while lowest number of Bills, only 2, was passed by Delhi, followed by Puducherry (3) and Mizoram (5). Lack of business is often cited as the reason for curtailing the duration of Assembly sessions.

In the Parliamentary system of governance that we are governed by, the legislature must act to enforce accountability of the executive to make governance responsible and people friendly. A feeble Legislature would give scope for an authoritarian Executive which would amount to change of the basic structure of the Constitutional framework. It is likely that a session could have a modest agenda for new legislations; but the Legislature need not cut short its sitting days for this reason. It must revisit the Rules and Procedures and bring in desirable modifications to keep Assembly running, and effectively, for a reasonably long period in a year. Question Hour could be made longer, greater use of Zero Hours, Call Attention Motions and Privilege Motions would add greater purpose to the Temple of Democracy.

It would not be proper to derive consolation that the situation in most other states is no better, even much worse. Odisha could take the lead and increase the number of sitting days to at least 100 through legislation. It needs to amend the Rules and Procedure to make greater use of the Zero Hours, Call Attention, and Question Hours. Bills need to be discussed in greater details; more recourse to Subject Committees would ensure quality evaluation of the Bills. Passage of Bills must not be rushed through. The prevailing impression that Legislators are in a hurry to close the session must end.

As things stand, any move to increase the salary and allowances of Legislators would not be taken kindly by the people. "Why should a Legislator get a highly liberal remuneration package when the Assembly sits for only 40 days in a year?" is a very valid reaction of a taxpayer. The proper arrangement should be our Assembly performs at a much higher level of productivity and our legislators get paid adequately. That would be in tune with the principle of 'Minimum Government and Maximum Governance'.

❑

Agniveers – our Nimble Soldiers

Battles are getting increasingly dependent on high-end technology. With this, the need for nimble soldiers today is greater than ever before. Major countries have been adopting different ways to forge harmony between sophisticated weapon systems and soldiers operating them. Countries are also steadily opting for a young armed force. India, too, has been alive to the need for reducing the average age of the men in uniform.

India's battlefields are varied and complex. These extend from glacial heights to coastal plains, from marshy lands to dense jungles, from hilly terrain to deserts. Our men at the border have been living in the most challenging weather conditions. They need to be of the right age and in perfect physical state to not only feel comfortable in freezing cold but remain agile enough to fight the adversary on the snow and win. Need for a young armed force has been felt since the Kargil Wars, Indian operations in Sri Lanka and during border confrontations with neighbouring countries and handling cross-border terrorists.

Huge share of the country's defence budget, however, is spent on the salary and pension of armed force personnel leaving a small share for capital acquisitions. This continuing imbalance needs correction. Induction of Agniveers addresses this critical issue. Some references of course have been made on the virtue of traditional recruitment on the basis of clan and there is a plea not to disturb this approach by inducting Agniveers from wider segments of society. It is true that for years, the Indian Army recruited men in large numbers from a few areas of the country where loyalty to the clan was predominantly noticed and was perceived as an asset for an effective Army. But subsequently the country opted for recruiting men from different states. Selection of Agniveers would only follow that pattern and therefore should not cause worry.

That the Government has revealed its determination to go ahead with the new scheme even while some political forces have been asking for a rollback of the arrangement, is a welcome development. Rightly, a clear message has also gone to agitators that doors of the Armed Forces are closed for those indulging in violence and destruction of property. Both the Centre and Armed Forces are now all set to operationalise the Agnipath scheme.

Is the new arrangement against the interest of the young job aspirants in the age group of 17-and-half to 21 years who would be joining the Armed Forces as Agniveers only for four years? Does it mean a letdown of the aspirations of those youths who dreamt of a career in the Armed Forces and earn pension after rendering the stipulated length of service?

This would appear as a serious human issue and needs a careful analysis. The Agniveers would be subject to selection for absorption in the Armed Forces after four years and 25 percent of them found suitable would continue in the Armed Forces. The rest would receive a reasonable amount as a severance package which would help the disengaged Agniveer in organising a new job for himself. In the meantime the government has reserved 10% of vacancies in Central Para Military Forces for the disengaged Agniveers. Many States have already come forward to recruit them for the state police as well. Public and Private sector enterprises are also positively inclined to engaging such candidates.

In the political cacophony following the announcement of the induction of Agniveers, some people have rushed with zeal to condemn the new arrangement. Diabolical plots had been scripted to torch railway coaches and to indulge in arson on a wide scale. People have been brought to the streets to agitate without many of them even knowing why they have been asked to agitate. It is significant that the government came out with clarification that the intake of Agniveers would progressively increase. This means, after four years, the society would steadily get enriched with larger number of well trained, disciplined young men and women who would add quality to the country's workforce whom the organised sector would be most willing to recruit.

There is a huge difference between a 40-year-old ex-serviceman and a 22-year-old ex-Agniveer in terms of employable qualities. Steady inflow of well trained and disciplined disengaged Agniveers into the society would surely impact the quality of country's youths in this age group and induce them to be more disciplined and productive– a huge social dividend our economy would benefit from.

The Armed Force of our country has always been a highly professional organisation, built over decades by sweat and blood of millions of brave and selfless soldiers who have dedicated their lives for the safety of the country and its countrymen. Its greatest asset has been its apolitical heart and its professional integrity and competence. How the Force would emerge more competent and remain ever battle ready is best left to be decided by our experts with the final call being taken by the political executive. Attempts to politicise the issue should be avoided. The merits of having a young armed force and a cost-effective Armed Force have been deliberated for years and finally Agniveers have emerged. The new Avatar represents a paradigm shift, and it needs to be welcomed rather than objected to.

❑

Growing Traffic Congestion in Bhubneswar

Traffic congestion has been a global urban phenomenon and with more vehicles hitting the city roads each year, the problem is more likely to get worse. It could have been otherwise if the mitigating measures were not prohibitively costly and were amenable to quick urban engineering solutions. The problem therefore would most likely linger on. While urban transport mix in developed countries is relatively simple, India's urban transport scenario continues to be much more complex, particularly in smaller cities.

A city like Bhubaneswar, for example, has to address the demands on the city roads of a large number of users. Many of them view the openness of the roads suitable to transact business and for social get together, while animals prefer to use the roads for rest and leisurely walk. City roads, replete with varieties of transport with different speed remain crowded.

How much time does a driver spend in a year waiting for traffic? In a city like Moscow, reportedly a driver spent 210 hours a year. In a city like Bangalore my guess is it could be about one and half times more. Being a much smaller city, Bhubaneswar has been facing the problem of slow traffic; also, traffic hold ups for quite some time. While some experts would pitch for more roads, more flyovers and even a mass rapid transit system like heavy rail, metro, subway, tube, or underground for solution, these are not feasible within a short time. There is the issue of availability of resources as well. Mass rapid transit system may not even be financially viable. We, therefore, need to adopt more pragmatic and feasible alternatives.

Roadblocks need to be addressed. There are too many of them. Street hawking has assumed menacing proportions. Much of the road space has been used for shopping and ancillary activities. Consequently, many existing roads now offer much less space for traffic to move.

As a first step, Bhubaneswar Municipal Corporation (BMC) needs to make certain important roads free from roadside shopping cabins and carts. The decision needs to be rigorously enforced and violations must attract heavy penalty. The city administration must ensure a zero-tolerance arrangement for stray cattle. Offending animals are to be presumed to be without owners and need to be swiftly confiscated, taken to Government Farm and sold off in public auction.

There are too many lanes meeting Main Roads. These intersections need rationalisation immediately and many could be closed. This exercise would facilitate smooth flow of traffic to some extent.

Number of motor bikes has increased exponentially. They too contribute to slowing down of traffic as most bikers seem to love their freedom and meander merrily on roads. Many prefer to wait on the left side of the road detaining the left bound traffic and as soon as the traffic light turns green, they swiftly turn right and speed away. This type of acrobatics must stop. There is urgency in having dedicated bike tracks and transgressions from the tracks must be penalised. Some road-cuts for convenience of a vehicle to take a "U" turn seem to act as bottlenecks and need to be widened to facilitate turning of vehicles without impacting the traffic flow.

Existing practice of seamless conversion of roadside buildings to commercial establishments is another area that has accentuated traffic congestion. These establishments attract a large number of vehicles which are parked on the roads and obstruct traffic. A well planned relocation drive must be initiated so that commercial establishments get located in a more orderly manner in designated zones, keeping arterial roads free for traffic to move faster. Similar to how stray animals are to be handled, zero tolerance must be ensured towards unauthorised parking of vehicles on roads.

These measures are feasible and would make the Capital City look cleaner, healthier, and more livable. The city thereby would look much more attractive for tourists and investors. We must resist the temptation of making the entire city a disorganised Bazaar.

❑

Our Youths and Panchayats

In the just concluded Elections, Odisha's 27.93 million rural voters were to elect 91,913 Ward Members, 6794 Sarpanches, 6793 Panchayat Samiti Members and 853 Zilla Parishad Members. As many as 189,099 candidates were in the fray, including 162,297 for Ward Members (1.76 candidates per seat), 34,613 for Sarpanches (5.09 candidates per seat), 3,999 for Zilla Parishad Members (4.68 candidates per seat) and 28,153 for Panchayat Samiti Members (4.14 candidates per seat). Prior to elections, expenditure limits for various offices were enhanced. For Zilla Parishad Members, it was enhanced to Rs 5 lakh from Rs 2 lakh and for Sarpanch, the raise was from Rs 80,000 to Rs 2 lakh.

About 210 lakh voters cast votes; 69 lakh voters did not. BJD polled 1,10,89,712 votes (52%); BJP 63,23,646 votes (30%) and Congress 28,54,398(13%). BJD won 765 seats in Zilla Parishad, an all time high– a rise of 289 seats in comparison to previous performance in 2017; BJP registered a steep slide from 297 in 2017 and could capture only 42 seats while Congress won 37 seats sliding down from 60 seats in 2017. So far, BJD's win has been the most spectacular in its over two decades of rule in Odisha. Interestingly, Panchayat Elections had generated a lot of interest and Opposition Parties had hoped to benefit from anti-incumbency sentiments.

In the run up to the Elections, interesting and encouraging signals had come out from different parts of the state that indicated a societal rethink on the quality of candidates and widespread use of inducement tactics to win votes. A village in Kutra Block of Sundargarh District decided to test Sarpanch aspirants to find out their suitability. Eight aspirants subjected themselves to the test. Youths of Ganiary village in Nuapada District launched a door to door campaign asking voters to keep themselves away from inducements and select a good person as Sarpanch. As Election date drew nearer, however, widespread use of various inducement tactics was reported. Reports of violence were disturbing, particularly about attacks on media men.

In their struggle for supremacy, political forces, however, have chosen to keep under the carpet the severe shortcomings and deficiencies Odisha's Gram Panchayats have been suffering from for years. Despite being the pivot for decentralised administration, they continue to be anemic and in frail health. Now that new Sarpanches have arrived, it may be timely to place before them a few important issues that continue to affect holistic development of the very important institution of the Gram Panchayat.

Considering the fact that Odisha has about close to 50,000 villages – next only to Uttar Pradesh and Madhya Pradesh, the number of Gram Panchayats remains too small. As a result, many Panchayats have a large number of villages, making satisfactory participation of the villagers in Gram Sabha meetings an impossible task. People's participation in the decision making process is key to a decentralised system of governance. Palli Sabha and Gram Sabha are institutions at the grassroots level through which annual budget proposals are routed and discussed, debated and approved. However, Palli Sabha doesn't meet regularly; Gram Sabhas have low participation. Proper recording of the minutes of meetings is not done. Participatory level of both the institutions is poor. Regular meetings of Standing Committees are not held. Proper records of meetings are not maintained. GPs are to prepare annual action plan and upload in the Plan Soft under e-panchayat. GPs make limited attempt to link their financial budget on the basis of resources at their disposal. Service delivery gap in different villages is hardly addressed. There is little coordination with functionaries of line departments. These persisting deficiencies are seldom addressed. Decentralised governance remains mostly on paper. GPs implement various development projects at village level but do not have adequate manpower. Shortage of essential manpower leads to severe malfunctioning of the GPs and heavy accumulation of unutilised Grants takes place.

Over decades, Panchayats have failed to generate adequate resources even though a large number of assets are owned by them. They have multifarious functions to discharge many of which could provide opportunities for generating resources. Precious little has been done in this area. The last State Finance Commission had observed that against transfer of funds from the Government of over Rs 8390 crore in 3 years from 2015-16, the own sources of revenue of Panchayati Raj Institutions (PRIs) was only Rs 100.86 crore (1.2%).

21 subjects out of 29 enlisted in Schedule XI of the Constitution have been devolved to the PRIs . These subjects include agriculture, land improvement, land reforms, land consolidation, soil conservation; minor irrigation, watershed development; dairy, poultry; minor forest produce; rural housing; drinking water; roads;

non-conventional energy sources; poverty alleviation programmes; primary education; markets and fairs; health and sanitation; public distribution; maintenance of public assets; social welfare; welfare of weaker sections. Adequate manpower is necessary for meaningful participation of GPs.

Like other Elections for PRIs, this year's Election too witnessed eagerness of candidates to spend huge sums of money for winning the office of Sarpanch. Electoral success through money power creates a compulsion for an adequate return on investment. PRIs provide many low hanging fruits in the shape of various opportunities to satisfy the craving for unmerited enrichment. Educated youths are, however, more likely to break this mindset and appreciate the potential Panchayati Raj holds . They can transform Panchayats into viable economic enterprises and ensure better quality of life to the rural population. They can remedy the systemic deficiencies of Palli Sabha and Gram Sabha; they would be able to ensure participation of most citizens in decision making.

India has many cases of rural transformation of astounding proportions through capable Sarpanches. With more and more educated young men and women now in the PRIs in Odisha, such wholesale transformation should be possible in different Districts.

Decoding Naveen Government's
New Variant Called 5T

People of Odisha are almost every day being sensitised with the arrival of a new era in governance after the introduction of 5T. There is not a single day when the newspapers do not carry news of the spread of 5T and the wonders it is doing in solving even the most challenging and most stubborn problems of the common man. It is therefore time, we genetically sequenced and decoded 5T-the new variant.

5T stands for (i) Teamwork, (ii) Technology, (iii) Transparency, (iv) Transformation and (v) Time-limit. As per government's new policy, all government action must be governed by these five cardinal principles. Any student of public administration would appreciate that these five ingredients constitute the core elements of democratic governance and governments, right from the time of independence, have been governed by such principles. The very fact that it is being rediscovered now by Naveen Government makes us suspect that these principles had vanished altogether during Naveen Patnaik's 22-year rule causing mass scale discontentment and erosion of popularity and being restored now to regain people's confidence. The vehemence with which it is being propagated is further proof that such principles are alien to most of the people in the government apparatus who deliver public service.

Technology, mostly IT, was introduced into governance in the late 80s. The world over, it enables citizens to access government services in a seamless manner from the comfort of their home. Most of the work can be done online.

But how does Odisha administration fare on this front? One still has to run to the RI office to pay land rent, though some lucky ones have been able to do it online. It is, however, still to become a universal experience. Imagine a situation where citizens are willing to pay but the government does not create the facility for an online payment. Will the 5T mandarins wake up to this and ensure this in a time-bound manner? Mutation case continues to be a low hanging fruit for the greedy land administration officials and people keep running to them to get their mutation cases disposed of. Almost regularly the State Vigilance catches a field official demanding and accepting bribe from the desperate citizen to get his mutation case disposed of.

Odisha government and the 5T variant have been overactive on the social media space to crowd it with government achievements. Regularly the Municipal Corporation's twitter handle provides photographs of streets and drains being cleaned. How real is such propaganda? The 5T variant is busy and active creating a surreal world which has severe 'disconnect' with ground reality. A good policy, on the other hand, should encourage citizens to take to social media to register their complaints and the authorities responding to such complaints.

What about transparency? The Kalinga Stadium was

spruced up for the World Cup Hockey Tournament and the event was organised in a grand way earning praise of the international community. By all standards it was a great success. But do we still know how much was spent on that event and who financed the project? Were transparency issues addressed? As per press reports, the real cost incurred on the lavish mansion called Kharavela Bhawan was not being reported for months by the executing department to the administrative department. Obviously, the issue of transparency was not being shown the respect it deserved. Government withheld the information on how much they spent fighting cases in High Court and Supreme Court in a case against Prakash Mishra, the former DG of Police. What was the great public interest sought to be achieved in sacrificing transparency in the instant case?

Similarly, the smart city project is being implemented with great fanfare. Do we know how much was spent and what was achieved with that huge expenditure? Why is a government, swearing by 5T, and not making voluntary disclosures on matters of public importance?

5T also talks about transformation. We should be clear about what we want to transform to. The Niti Ayog periodically tracks the performance of various states in achievement of Sustainable Development Goals (SDG). SDG aims at reduction of poverty, hunger, ensuring health-care, good education, gender equality, clean water etc. Odisha's rank slipped from 15th to 19th during 20-21. Odisha slipped two places to 14th spot in the overall health index prepared by the Niti Ayog. Odisha slipped to the 29th position in the ease of doing business.

The Public Affairs Center prepares a Public Affairs Index wherein State Governments are evaluated on five themes - effectiveness of government, control over corruption, accountability, rule of law and regulatory equality. Odisha ranks 17th in that index, below UP. Is this the transformation that 5T seeks to achieve?

5T seeks to enforce 'time-limit' on delivery of services. To retain credibility, it must adhere to time limits for normal requirements of citizens. Why do mutation cases remain pending indefinitely? Why do allegations of heavy bribe for finalising mutation cases keep coming in? The real test of 5T would be to gauge how far it has succeeded in making the life of a citizen easier. Time and cost overruns on major development projects have become the rule rather than exception. The completion schedule for the Bus Terminal at Baramunda remains open. While foundation laying for a project becomes an expensive government festival, no importance is given to when a project would be completed and at what cost. Potholes on city roads seem to enjoy immortality, so do hawkers on pavements.

Official portal of Government of Odisha on 5T states that teamwork, technology, transparency, transformation and time limit will be the five factors on which performance of government officials and projects will be judged. It also states that adherence to 5T charter is now the top priority of the Odisha government for which a separate Department has been created. This all important Department seems to have messed up fundamental principles of an Organisation like Unity of Command and Hierarchical System. Primacy of the Secretary to the Government in the affairs of his Department has been severely compromised. Even the primacy of the Chief Secretary seems to have been dented.

The ubiquitous 5T model of the Naveen Patnaik Government is akin to the elephant for blind men, with different meaning to different people. It appears on the wall of a renovated school building, it also appears on a street hydrant. Despite relentless publicity on 5T, malfeasance in governance runs galore. Decline in standards of governance and publicity drive on 5T seem to be running parallel. 5T is an English abbreviation and is interpreted in different ways by the Aam Admi of the state. It seems it never was meant to enrich the quality of governance; its purpose seems to be to create hype which political managers think would work during elections.

❏

Little Odia Content on Internet

National Education Policy, inter alia, refers to India's extremely rich literature in classical languages like Sanskrit, Tamil, Telugu, Kannada, Malayalam, Odia and emphasises on the need for preservation of the priceless works along with the immortal works of other languages like Pali, Persian, Prakrit for enrichment of posterity and hopes that future generations would benefit from such classical literature. Such resources will also be widely available in schools, possibly, as online modules through innovative approach.

The policy document describes how Sanskrit contains vast treasures of Mathematics, Medicine, Architecture, Philosophy, Grammar, Music, Metallurgy, Drama, Poetry and Story-telling and how this wide spectrum of knowledge is known as Sanskrit Knowledge System. The policy document says it would be offered at all levels of school and higher education as an important enriching option for students. But for this to happen, India needs to break the present meagre 0.01% Indian language content presence on the internet.

Why we have near nonexistent content presence on the internet needs a discussion. In 2020, Indian language computing completed the 50th year. The first integrated Devanagari computer was developed in 1983. Indian scripts encoding standard ISCII (Indian Script Code for Information Interchange) along with keyboard layout standard INSCRIPT were officially released by BIS (Bureau of Indian Standards) in 1988. This standard was developed by a group of scientists at IIT Kanpur who studied all major Indo-Aryan scripts, their behavior, the needs for computing and evolved the standard over a period of one and half decades. The ISCII standard document released by BIS was not a list of characters alone. It covered every aspect of the script properties, outlined the principles and rules that must govern the script behaviors in computing such that the implementation was unambiguous and efficient.

Text display is the technology needed to make the digital representation into visual readable representation. The font display formats are defined by Microsoft and Adobe and released as the OpenType standard. This standard does not implement Odia script rules and therefore, creates ambiguous rendering. For example, ◉+6Ol is same as ◉+6O+Ol. This results in a lot of ambiguous text creation which is not searchable or processed by algorithms for machine learning or text processing. Moreover, the format is so complex that even Adobe's own PDF software does not implement it. That makes all Odia PDF documents nonstandard and non-searchable and non-quotable. The complexity of this font format also made it impossible for calligraphers to design fonts for Odia, due to which, the publishers cannot create searchable digital content. Those Indian language publishers who exist, use legacy nonstandard software.

Odia character set needed standardisation. The Odia support we see today, however, is governed by the Unicode consortium and the state of Odisha has no guidelines. While Odia is taught and learnt the same way for all students of Odia in schools, what gets implemented on computers is different. The number of characters in Odia Unicode over the years has been changing. They make it to the software we use on our phones and computers. But the students of today learning from Barnabodha or their teachers, parents learnt the same Odia letters that did not have to evolve; whereas Odia users on computers and phones confuse with characters in Unicode every day.

We may not be in a position to, or, may not gather enough motivation to change the input hardware (the keyboard) which had been designed for English language only and has been then adopted for other languages across the world. However, comparing English typing with Odia, is an unfair comparison. Today, in the field of writing, Odia users are a lot more comfortable with pen and paper than a keyboard; whereas, it is the opposite with English users. So, it will be natural that Odia use will remain confined to paper and pen.

Since OpenType format was designed for use with Unicode text and Unicode omitted the properties and characteristics of the characters encoded, OpenType failed to make an unambiguous definition of the rules to be applied. That made the design of fonts in different languages extremely complex and still unreliable.

Odia writing is learnt in 3 steps. The Barnamala, the matras and the juktakshars. How these three steps translate into "typing" needs to be taught and practised. Since we do not have digital literacy in schools nor do we have a standard input method for mobile phones or tablets for Odia, all users are forced to look at a QWERTY English keyboard and try to figure out how to type Odia. A native Odia keyboard on mobile or tablets also does not implement the three steps.

India had started creating digital content since late 1980s and grew to digital publishing in a decade. Internet came in 1995 but didn't support Indian languages for about 15 years. All legacy content became incompatible with Unicode. So, we have little content on the internet.

It is necessary to effect required architectural changes in the existing Operating Systems, so that indigenous innovation in language tools like spell checkers/ grammar checkers can be freely integrated. This will also facilitate larger Indian language-content on the internet. This is also the way to preserve our languages.

This very important matter has been badly delayed. It is sheer fallacy to access the Knowledge domain on the Internet only through English language. This will deprive millions of Indians of advantage of Internet through their own language. Surely none would like that. It is time State Government and Government of India jointly examined the issues involved and took up the matter with Unicode for a satisfactory resolution of the technical issues.

❑

Rooftop Solar Power Generation in Odisha Continues to be Slow

India is the world's fourth biggest emitter of carbon dioxide after China, the US and the EU. In the COP26 at Glasgow, Prime Minister Narendra Modi announced India's resolve to get 50% of its energy from renewable resources by 2030, and, by the same year, to reduce total projected carbon emissions by one billion tons and emissions intensity of the GDP by 45%. India stands committed to 500 gigawatts (GW) of non-fossil electricity capacity by 2030.

With more than 300 days of clear sunny days, India has been working on a target of 40GW (40,000MW) of on-grid Rooftop Solar Projects (without battery) on residential, commercial and institutional establishments. RTS 1 (Rooftop Solar Scheme Phase 1) was operational till March 2019. State Nodal Agencies were authorised to disburse subsidy to all segments of customers except commercial establishments. DISCOMs/State Utilities were to give the permission for Solar Net-meter installation for these rooftop projects so that a consumer having generation through his rooftop installation can get credit for generation and pay energy charge only for the amount in excess of what he generated. This impacted revenue of DISCOMs/State Utilities. MNRE thereafter formulated RTS 2 (Roof-top Solar Scheme Phase 2) where the DISCOMs/State Utilities were given responsibilities to disburse subsidy only to Residential rooftop solar PV.

DISCOMS/State Utilities were to give permission for the Net-metering. For such activities, DISCOM/state utility would be incentivised by Government of India. This led to proliferation of roof-top solar projects across the country but Odisha was left behind even after a compulsory allocation of 4 MW of roof-top solar projects by MNRE for residential units (1MW each for all the four DISCOMs in Odisha) during October 2019. Not a single case of subsidy has been disbursed by the DISCOMs due to various reasons including transitional and transformational activities, such as recovery from damage suffered by CESU from Cyclone Fani and subsequent take-over of DISCOMs by Tata Power. MNRE advised GRIDCO to coordinate and push the scheme in Odisha. Finally, OREDA, the State Nodal Agency for Renewable Energy in Odisha, empanelled vendors and all DISOCMs (TPCODL, TPNODL, TPWODL and TPSODL) agreed to take over the subsidy disbursement activity as per MNRE's original provision and methodology mentioned in RTS 2 scheme.

Since then, however, there has been little activity and even after two years of allocation of 4MW capacity by MNRE, Odisha has not been able to disburse subsidy to any of the residential consumers in Odisha. No government intervention by Department of Energy which could have taken suitable actions against the DISCOMs has been forthcoming.

In the meantime, many states have moved fast in the area of rooftop solar installations. Gujarat tops the list of states with the highest installed rooftop solar energy generation capacity in India with total rooftop solar capacity as on 31st August, 2021 at 1357 MW. Maharashtra comes next, with 765 MW. Rajasthan has the third-highest installed rooftop solar capacity at 543 MW followed by Haryana at 349 MW. Next performer is Tamil Nadu with 334 MW, followed by Karnataka at 295MW. Uttarakhand with 262 MW comes next followed by Uttar Pradesh with 259MW. Delhi has a capacity at 201 MW followed by Telangana at 199 MW. Odisha stood at the 22nd place with a capacity of only 19 MW. India's total capacity stood at 5484 MW.

As on March 31, 2021, Odisha had 79.77 lakh domestic consumers and 6.20 lakh Kutir Jyoti consumers. Total LT consumers were 92.79 lakhs. In 2019-20, Odisha's 88.4 lakh LT consumers were billed by DISCOMs for around Rs 4880 crore. This worked out to Rs 5430 per annum or Rs 452 per month for power consumption per consumer. Actual collection however was only Rs 3529 crore and per consumer realisation was Rs 3992 per annum or Rs 333 per month. This indicates that on an average, a LT consumer consumed per month electric energy worth Rs 450 per month which at the then tariff was around 120 units of electricity. Tariff has been rising and a consumer today would pay Rs 2030 for 400 units a month, and Rs 3270 for 600 units. With 300 days of productive working in a year, a rooftop Solar PV of 3 KW would generate 3600 units per year or 300 units per month. The consumer by having this rooftop device could save at the current tariff Rs 1480 per month. Cost of a 3 KW rooftop solar PV to the customer would be around Rs 1.80 lakh and subsidy available from Government of India is Rs 15,000 up to 3 KW and Rs 7600 for capacity between 4 and 10 KW. Unfortunately, Odisha has not been able to utilise any subsidy allocation for two years and rooftop programme for residential purpose has come to a halt.

World, however, is getting sensitised to the need for reducing carbon emission and more and more homes are going solar. Many cities have now well-articulated policy to make this happen within a time-frame. For example, city of Berlin recently decided that new buildings and significant rooftop renovations will have mandatory solar PV, both for residential and non-residential buildings. This program is expected to turn 30% of all Berlin roofs into solar roofs. Within the first five years of the program, this decision could save approximately 37,000 tons of CO_2 every year.

So far, the state has done little in this area. 19 MW capacity on rooftop facilities by now is mostly on institutional buildings. At the most, 2000 such buildings would have been covered by now. Residential units have been so far left out. Out of close to 80 lakh domestic consumers of electricity, Odisha has at least ten lakh homes who would be having high-energy use gadgets like room air-conditioners. These consumers should be interested in having rooftop facilities. One lakh houses out of this group with rooftop solar PV would create a capacity of 300 MW and could contribute to reduction of carbon emission of good measure. That no such clear guidelines are forthcoming from government is perplexing. That inaction of the DISCOMS over two years in operationalising the subsidy facility does not even has any impact on government is disturbing.

Odisha needs an immediate clear and bold policy and it must demonstrate its ability to respond to India's commitment to reduction of carbon emission and increased use of non-fossil power. It is necessary that rooftop solar facility should be incentivised adequately by the state government through a new scheme.

❏

Ragi Cultivation in Odisha

India's five major millet-producing states are Karnataka, Maharashtra, Uttar Pradesh, Haryana and Rajasthan. Among millets, Bajra accounts for the largest production (about 11 million MT) which is over 60% of India's total millet production (18 million MT). Jowar is the second largest millet crop, contributing about 5 million MTs accounting for over 26.5% of total millet production. Ragi (Finger Millet), known as Mandia in Odisha, has a share of 12% to total millet production of the country. India produces about 2 million MTs of Ragi. Only two percent of the total millet production is from small millets. Eighty percent of Asia's millet production is from India. India's global share is about 20%. Up to 1965-70, India's millet production contributed 20% to country's food basket. Over a period of time, however, production of wheat and rice increased while production of millets dwindled. Now millets contribute about 6% of the food basket.

Odisha produces very small quantity of millets. Largest contribution comes from Ragi with the crop grown in 1.17 lakh hectare. Total production of Ragi is 1.29 lakh MT with productivity at 1102 kg per hectare. Odisha contributes 2.15% to country's Ragi production while Karnataka, the largest producer, accounts for over 66%, followed by Tamil Nadu (11.07%) and Uttarakhand 8.73%. Area under Bajra and Jowar in Odisha is negligible. Rice is, however, grown in Odisha in over 39 lakh ha. State production in 2019-20 was 96.37 lakh MT and productivity was 2453 kg/ha.

It would be worth examining the land-use pattern of the state's croplands and then assess the extent to which Ragi could spread in Odisha. The state has a geographical area of 155.71 lakh ha of which total cultivated land is about 61.80 lakh ha (39.69%). Of the 61.80 lakh ha of cultivated area, 29.14 lakh ha is highland (47%), 17.55 lakh ha (28%) is medium land and 15.11 lakh ha (25%) is low land. Paddy is grown in 6.66 lakh ha of high land, 15.88 lakh ha medium land and 13.94 lakh ha of low land. Gross cropped area of the state is 82.01 lakh ha. In 2018-19, Paddy accounted for 46.28% of the gross cropped area, Millets 1.92%, Pulses 23.40%, Oil seeds 7.08%, Cotton 1.89%, Potato 0.30%, Sugarcane 0.30% and Fruits and other crops 15.60%.

Millet coverage of gross cropped area in Odisha has been varying from time to time. While it was 5.2% in 1970-71, it was 8.49% in 80-81, but declined to 3.67% in 90-91, 3.13% in 2000-01, 2.29 in 2010-11 and only 1.92 % in 2018-19. Reduction of area under millet in Odisha over a period of time has been over 75%. A mission-mode drive should aim at covering up to 5% of the gross cropped area with emphasis on improved productivity mainly through improved seeds.

Odisha has been procuring huge quantity rice from producers at MSP and making available sufficient quantity under public distribution system at one rupee per kg. This arrangement has been reaching nook and corner of the state. Food preference of the people of the state for decades has been overwhelmingly rice and wheat-based. In this situation how Ragi, the predominant millet of the state, would emerge as the staple food even for a small segment of state's population is not clear.

It is however true that Ragi has many characteristics that could make it eminently suitable for adoption as the preferred crop for high land farmers in rain deficit non-irrigated areas of the state. Requirement of water for Ragi is the lowest (350 mm) among crops like Maize (500 mg), Sorghum (400 mm), Wheat (650 mm) and Rice (1250 mm). Gluten free, high on calcium, protein, Vitamin A, Vitamin B and Phosphorus, and with its high fibre content, Ragi could be the preferred food for many. Its resilience to climate change makes it a contingent crop. Its adaptability to harsh climate conditions has made it grow in the coastal region around Kanyakumari as well as in the Himalayan foothills of Uttarakhand.

Odisha started with the Millet Mission in 2017 in 30 blocks in 7444 acres covering 8043 farmers. It was extended to 84 blocks in 15 districts and will cover 142 blocks in 19 districts in 2022-23. There is talk of even scaling up the spread to all 314 Blocks of the state. For the programme to succeed, many issues, however, need to be addressed. These mainly relate to productivity and its acceptance by farmers as the preferred crop over competing crops like Cotton, Niger, Maize and Tree crops. It, however, looks highly unlikely that it would be an acceptable alternative to Rice under public distribution system and even in midday meal programme in schools. With increase in production, these issues would pose more serious challenge. It is also unlikely that even the rural consumers would give up widely accepted snacks like Pakoda, Bara, Maggi or Samosa in favour of Ragi based cookies. Even greater consumer resistance is likely in urban areas. It could possibly emerge as an occasional heath food in some high-end urban households.

Another serious issue relates to the needs of the state's farmer. Whether Ragi would ensure adequate return to make a farmer voluntarily give up his option to take up cotton or maize or niger farming needs to be examined carefully. Moreover, is Government paying the same attention to other crops which look more crucial and a lot more remunerative? Chironji, for example, is a valuable produce which people collect from forests and sell. With adequate support, Chironji crop can be grown along the edge of the farmer's plots. A farmer could earn over a lakh of rupees annually by selling the seeds. Mohua Tree would provide useful cattle-feed. Its promotion on farmer's land is yet to be a government programme. Promotion of non-edible oilseed plantations is yet to be started in the state.

An Odisha rural household needs Onion with Pakhala and would welcome adequate supply of home-grown Onion. Widely held perception is only 15% of the state's requirement is now met through local production. Potato Mission has been a great failure. The state needs exponential growth of production of Pulses that would provide higher return to the farmers. By promoting Drum-Stick in villages and even in urban kitchen gardens, we could provide a renewable source of highly nutritional food to Odisha households. This simple solution to Odisha's persisting malnutrition problem has not been adopted. These important issues need to be taken up urgently and, in tandem, with promotion of Millets.

Just as Punjab could produce enough Rice and Wheat and contributed substantially to the country's buffer stock, it should be possible for a state like Karnataka or Karnataka and Tamil Nadu together, to grow enough Finger Millet for meeting the emerging needs of this wonder crop. Most states perhaps need not take up the programme with the same zeal neglecting more pressing demands of other crops. A holistic approach would help.

❑

People I Come Across in Daily Life

He would consult me on phone before he deducted some amount towards Income Tax from my monthly pension. I too have his phone number. Once I called him to find out when he would be available in the Bank. I was surprised when he said he had retired months ago, and, therefore, went to the Bank around twelve thirty. I was impressed. But I was in for more surprise. He was not alone. The Man Friday in the Bank, whom I always looked forward to for every odd thing – like, having a new cheque book, getting cash from my account, updating my passbook-- I understood only that day, was also someone who had retired two years ago. I know only these two such officials who have been sharing their long experience with the personnel working at present in that Branch of the Bank. There could be even more such men whom I do not know. I asked the Manager if these two retired men were engaged on contract. They, I was told, worked for free. It was a case of someone giving back to the society. They stood out as exception to the prevailing craze of many for sinecures on retirement, for more emoluments and more perks. One of those two would ring up from the Bank and tell me that the arrears of my enhanced pension had just been credited to my account. Normally I would have received a message to this effect on my phone from the Bank. There are some people in every organisation who loved to walk an extra mile to make others happy. That is why a smile perhaps still lurks in our world amidst plenty of tears.

On the 11th April, 2014 my young Banker friend, Satya, left Bhubaneswar on transfer to Vijayawada. He never had a posting in Andhra, his home state. For last six months I have been noticing his anxiety over his posting. His only child, a son, must complete his school study in Andhra, he told me once, to be eligible for studying in Andhra based educational institution of his choice. The son was not prepared to live in Andhra in their ancestral house with his mother unless his father was with him. At last, his prayer had been answered. This young man, Satya, would never let me to go to the Bank for transacting my business. He would come to my house with all necessary papers for me to put my signature on; even carry my passbook for updating. He was a mobile Bank for me. Always smiling, he would come on many occasions even at eight in the evening. He would share his moments of anxiety with me if the annual deposit target was proving difficult to reach. One day I insisted on knowing his blood pressure as he looked sick. He never checked it, he said. Here was a nice professional, so dedicated to his job, working for hours for the Bank, well educated, got into the profession through a competitive examination and yet was so indifferent to his health !! I was annoyed. I sent him to the doctor who lived in the outhouse. He checked his Blood Pressure and found it all right. I was happy. "I have a good friend, a doctor, in Vijayawada", I told him and advised him to get in touch with him. He has agreed. I once said, Satya, I would miss you." He smiled and said, " my successor would be even better."

On 23rd July, 2014, I had a firsthand experience of a customer being the King. I had been to a local Branch of a

Nationalised Bank to close my Savings Bank Account. The Manager received me with a smile, got up from his chair and offered me a seat. He smiled even when he knew I had come to close my Account. He looked at my application and promptly escorted me to another room and made me settle down comfortably while he instructed the concerned person and assured me that my work would be attended to. It seemed to me as if all other activities in the Bank were kept on hold till I was handed over my balance amount in cash. The cashier suggested I counted it before putting the cash into my briefcase. "There is no need", I said smiling. "I was counting while you did it thrice" I said. He smiled. I saw the benign Manager again in his chamber and promised him to see him occasionally even though I have closed my account. He smiled. I walked into my car wondering if such decent people would soon be extinct or efficiency and courtesy would win in my country.

Let me write about another experience. It was September 27, 2014 when I had a pleasant experience with efficiency in a public office. I went to the Personal Banking Branch of a Public Sector Bank in Bhubaneswar along with daughter and her husband. I took a seat that was vacant. I did not know if the official at the desk dealt with matters I was trying to sort out. My daughter and her husband joined me. The officer in charge of the seat listened to our requirements. Each of us had different work. She attended to all our issues by going from one desk to another. She would swiftly go even to the Chief Manager for consultation; the Chief Manager would come to us to seek further clarification. While attending to our complex requirements, she would attend to a few other customers as well. She would get a few documents of us photocopied in-house. We left the counter after about one and half hours.

All our needs had been met. The pleasure was that while we remained seated, she moved from place to place and rendered service to us. My son-in-law wondered if he had ever been served so efficiently by any executive of the new generation Banks where he has accounts. I thanked her while leaving and wondered if even a dedicated single window system was ever as effective anywhere in my country.

There must be very good reasons why my Insurer wants my Life Certificate every year for one policy and my Live Certificate once in five years for another. For persons like me, however, it only causes bewilderment. Instead of wasting my time knowing the reason and get a bit wiser, I present myself in the office, as per the requirement and I am happy about it. What I was not happy about is what i would now like to write on.

On the 29th August, 2017, I went to the insurance office and my familiarity with the layout of the office hall made me walk into the cubicle I went to the previous year. I sat before the presiding officer who, I thought, was sitting idle and was not even looking at the computer before him. I noticed some reluctance in his eyes to meet mine but when they did, I spoke about Life Certificate. The presiding deity just stretched his left hand towards the next cubicle. I turned my face to the right and saw through the glass wall the presiding deity talking on phone while a quiet white-haired slim lady was sitting before her. Before moving, I asked the presiding officer if he could help me in correcting my address in their records. He was courteous enough to admit that he knew nothing about Life Certificate or issues related to it. I moved and made myself comfortable on a chair before the presiding officer in the next cubicle, beside the quiet lady.

The presiding officer sounded sincere on phone and looked anxious to fix the problem she was talking about. I admired her silently for that. The lady visitor, I thought, was getting all attention . The officer finished her chat on phone and a moment later responded to yet another call. I waited and used the time filling the form so that I would be ready to present it to her for her endorsement as soon as she was free from the telephone. She looked at me and I said I had come for the Life Certificate. She immediately stretched her hand towards the door and told me to go to the person sitting "just there". I was no wiser; but went to the empty space outside the door and gazed at the Hall of Insensitivity.

Someone I unwittingly was standing close to, spoke to me and wanted to help. Knowing my requirement, he offered me a chair and asked me to wait for the person who would come back to his seat within minutes. I waited and found a person on the next chair looking at me rather closely. Our eyes met and he blurted out my father's name. I told him my name. He smiled and remembered both my father and me. He too was waiting for the Life Certificate. The person in demand, at last, walked in and took his seat. The person, who had enquired about my father, whispered some words into the ear of the official who would do the job. This made the official look at me. He said my face was a familiar one. But his next question baffled me. He asked me if I was in the Police. I said I wasn't and then he asked me if I was not the Author of Asura (Demon). I was aghast. I said I did write occasionally; but never on Demons. He apologised and said Asura was not related to demon but is a great novel. I quietly handed him the form. He wanted a proof of identity. I showed him my Aadhar Card. He said my job was done.

Now I was in for more surprise. I saw the white-haired lady again. She was now seated on the chair I had just vacated and was requesting for a Life Certificate. I realised the poor lady was in fact waiting before the lady official in vain. I was both sad and angry that the lady official on phone was not attending to her problem on phone as I thought; but was talking on phone about something else and made the poor lady waste her time.

I remembered my experience last year. My job then had been done almost in minutes by an official in one of those two cubicles I visited this time. What I realised this time is the insurance company had put there this year two persons who were extremely low on sensitivity.

❑

A Page from my Friend's Childhood

Can you recount any adventure in your childhood? I once asked my friend, Gopal. He had lost his mother when he was a small child and, like many children placed in similar situation, was reared by the father who was over possessive. A father in such a situation created in himself a kindly mother for young child. Gopal was eight years old and the family's Man Friday, Kunjia, for Gopal was the most capable person on the earth. Kunjia would work in the field; sow paddy; harvest the crop; tend the cattle, manage the manure pit; run an errand; and, even catch fish when catch is easy in Kimiria river close to Gopal's village Baniari in Barchana Block of Jajpur District. The village is near Balia village, home of the celebrated Odia poet of the 18th century, Abhimanyu Samanta Singhar.

Inquisitive Gopal yearned to learn catching Pohala fish from the flowing Kimiria the way Kunjia did. "Can you make a Polua for me? Not a big one like yours. I want a smaller one that I can handle"; Gopal had requested Kunjia. Polua is a fish catching device made of flexible reeds tied like a cross with a piece of cloth tied to the four ends of the reeds. Polua is to be placed into the water by two swift hands when the prying eyes notice movement of the unseen Pohala cruising like a submarine. The Polua is lifted as dexterously as it is lowered.

On an important afternoon, while Gopal's father was having his midday siesta and obedient Gopal was lying near him, daydreaming his exploits in the Kimiria, Kunjia arrived quietly and showed the tiny Polua, specially made for Gopal. It had the same effect on him as Krishna's flute had on Radha. He too, like Radha, left home on the sly and Kunjia led the way.

Sensing emptiness in the bed, Gopal's father soon realised that his tender child was missing. He apprehended the worst and looked at every corner of the house. Gopal's sister-in-law would not tell a lie to her father-in-law when asked if she had seen the child. "Gopal has gone to the river with Kunjia." she said. The angry father waited with a cane. An elated Gopal returned with a kilogram of Pohala-- his own catch-- at his maiden attempt. Instead of appreciation, he got a couple of smart lashings and the wailing child dropped his catch on the floor. He was made to promise to his father that cruel afternoon that he will never be a fisherman but would study well.

Gopal kept his promise. He did not catch fish thereafter; but grew up to love fish curry. Even now I would see smiling Gopal on his scooter go past me on many mornings telling me that he was on his way to the fish market.

❑

Witnessing Birth of Cynicism

I saw him regularly in the morning on the lane, walking either in the same direction or in the opposite direction. We didn't know each other. After some days, however, our eyes met but the encounter remained a brief affair, without any communication. Then the eyed decided to meet longer and speak. After some days, the meetings had their effect on our face. We exchanged smile and felt drawn to each other.

He was perhaps much younger but walked with greater attention on the road. Finally, we broke silence and spoke to each other. The talk continued to be brief for many days, but it became a regular feature.

He seemed to be a responsible citizen, concerned about garbage-free lanes, smooth roads-- free of potholes, functional footpaths, storm-water drains without obstructions. One day he disclosed how he , till a year ago, soon after his morning walk, would contact regularly the municipal authorities on civic deficiencies he noticed in his area .After some years he became aware that his persistent efforts were not being taken kindly. He realised he was considered as an obstinate person, a complaining man.

He learnt the hard way and made peace with deficiency. I felt sorry; but couldn't tell him whether it was right to be a concerned citizen. We gradually started walking together. After walking some distance with me, he would take a different turn and then would be home bound. Our meetings after many months became sporadic.

A few days ago, I saw him again he was walking slowly. He surely was having a problem on his right leg. I felt concerned. He spoke to me on the issue. He had sprained his leg while walking, perhaps absent minded. The right leg had got into a pothole. I was sad. He came out with a weird explanation. He said, "I know, even inanimate objects like pebbles in potholes, the garbage, the iron pipes dumped on the footpath, the abandoned wooden cabins on the side of lanes, the abandoned cars and jeeps in the roadside automobile repair shop, too have minds of their own. They know persons who are kind to them, love them and their sympathisers and who are not. They love their patrons and punish their enemies. One day a pothole must have decided to teach me a lesson and that is the reason it made me trip and fall into it." I looked at him in disbelief. Cynicism was writ large on his face. I realised how an insensitive work-culture wrecked havoc on a healthy mind.

❑

Fasting During Eclipse

Intermittent fasting is observed in various religious practices, including Buddhism, Christianity, Hinduism, Islam, Jainism and Judaism. Such fasting has been useful for blood sugar management, it helped disease prevention, improved brain function, delayed ageing, supported growth and metabolism and helped body weight management. It is an evolved art of living and reflected a person's rational rather than emotional attitude to food. It made a person more resolute; low on anger, it controlled mood and helped in viewing food as a necessary input for health rather than an object for indulgence.

In our society, fasting is also associated with certain special occasions of religious significance like Ekadasi and Sankranti. Sun and Moon have been intimately connected with human lives since the arrival of human beings on earth. Man has been worshipping the Sun since time immemorial. Sun has been viewed as the prime reason for life in this world. Planets revolve in their predetermined path around the Sun; Sun is responsible for rain. Man has been invoking Sun's grace to enlighten him, sharpen his intelligence, and acquire the power of discrimination. Moon has been viewed as the controller of man's mood, his emotions. These two celestial bodies have been worshipped as the manifestation of the Divine. When they suffer an eclipse, there is widespread concern for good and valid reasons.

The devotee practices austerities and awaits the eclipse to be over to resume normal activities.

It would be sheer ignorance to view fasting during eclipse as a superstitious ritual without carefully studying the impact of eclipse on the earth. Photovoltaic energy generated on the eclipse day is found to be reduced substantially in comparison to that on a clear-sky day. A solar eclipse is a natural phenomenon that results in an abrupt and short-time perturbation of the solar radiation reaching the area of its visibility on the Earth's surface. Such an event results in noticeable and important terrestrial consequences in the atmosphere.

A solar eclipse poses a challenge for power system of any country that has high percentage of solar power integration to grid. Researchers at Banaras Hindu University found that a solar eclipse on 21 June 2020 caused a substantial decrease in solar irradiance reaching the earth. At its peak, an eclipse cuts earth's surface ozone levels substantially. The eclipse also cools earth's atmosphere, changing temperature, relative humidity and wind speed. These changes have been most marked during the peak of the eclipse. Eclipse has been found to cause significant decrease in wind speed. Winds also blew more southerly in the shadowed regions. That the eclipse influences temperature and also causes the wind to drop speed and change direction has been documented.

In such a state of disturbance in the earth affecting wind speed, its direction, earth's temperature and reduction of heat, reduced availability of energy and dip in ozone level, it is foolhardy to imagine that human body would remain unaffected during such a phenomenon. Human body has to have a rational response to counter the adverse effects of such disturbances. Fasting, therefore, has been resorted to as a defensive response to protect human health.

The self-styled rationalists seem to behave most irrational when they resort to public display of gluttony when the need of the hour is to abstain from food. The other relevant issue is their love for non-vegetarian food. Meat consumption has been found to be responsible for releasing greenhouse gases such as methane, carbon dioxide, and nitrous oxide. These gases contribute to climate change including global warming.

Livestock farming contributes to these greenhouse gases in several ways. It destroys forest ecosystems because livestock farming has necessitated destroying large forest tracts by burning and thus releasing enormous amounts of CO2 into the atmosphere. Raising of cows and sheep create large amounts of methane as they digest food. The manure that ruminant animals produce also releases methane. Many types of fertilizers used in soybean production are nitrogen-based, and these lead to nitrous oxide emissions. Meat industry has been found to be unsustainable as animal livestock uses large amount of land resources. It has been found that despite using 77 per cent of agricultural land; only 17pc of global caloric consumption comes from animals. Yet in 2019 alone, an estimated 325 million metric tons of meat was produced. It takes a lot of water to produce meat. There is plenty of science and research to back up the conclusion that meat consumption has an adverse impact on environment.

Indians' fasting immediately prior to and during eclipse is, therefore, a social practice based on science and rationality and the so-called rationalists publicly displaying gluttony during eclipse are exhibiting nothing other than crude irrationality.

❑

Too Many Small Villges in Odisha

More than sixty eight per cent of India's population lived in 5,97,618 inhabited villages. Out of them, 37,439 villages didn't have 3G/4G mobile internet services. At 8947, Odisha has the maximum number of such villages. Uttar Pradesh, with the highest rural population of 155 million accounting for 18.6% of country's rural population, had 97,813 inhabited villages while Odisha had a rural population of 35 million accounting for only 4.4% of country's rural population but had 47,677 inhabited villages. Madhya Pradesh with 58 million (6.3% of country's rural population) had 51,929 villages. Odisha has the third largest number of villages in India, next only to Uttar Pradesh and Madhya Pradesh. While the average number of people per village was 1394 for India, it was 1503 for Maharastra, 1389 for Karnataka, 1862 for Gujarat, 1380 for Uttar Pradesh, 1013 for Madhya Pradesh and 734 for Odisha.

Kotagarh Block of Kandhamal district in Odisha, as per Census 2011 figures, comprises 133 villages out of which 17 villages have a population below 100. The least populated village Nuasajeli has only 2 inhabitants. Malaguda village has only 13 people. Kerpai Gram Panchayat in Thuamul Rampur block of Kalahandi district has as many as 31 villages with the largest village Majhigaon having 382 people. Salebali village had only 20 inhabitants, Taijhola, only 17 and Champajuan village had 50 people.

India's 5,97,518 inhabited villages had 2,38,054 Gram Panchayats (December 2010 figures). This works out to each Grama Panchayat having 2.5 villages. In respect of Odisha, however, the average works out to 7 villages per Gram Panchayats while it is 1.88 for Uttar Pradesh, 2.26 for Madhya Pradesh and 1.47 villages for Maharashtra.

Many states have opted for a Gram Panchayat for one village or around 2 to 3 villages. Such an arrangement has made Gram Sabha more representative of the Panchayat. A Panchayat having 20 villages can hardly have inhabitants of every village attending a meeting of the Gram Sabha. Inhabitants of distant villages generally lose many benefits of various development activities.

In July 2016, 19 children died of malnutrition in Nagada village of Jajpur district that drew the attention of local and national media. The revenue village had three hamlets located on hills within two kilometers from one another. Basic facilities like road, electricity, drinking water, mobile phone network, health facilities were lacking.

After the wide media coverage of the malnutrition deaths, Government constituted a Task Force comprising senior bureaucrats to look after the developmental works. Construction of road, provision of drinking water, construction of school and Anganwadi buildings, facility of electricity, etc. were taken up. Now physical amenities have, to some extent, improved; but the small habitations remain vulnerable to distress situations.

Even today, cases of human miseries keep surfacing from vulnerable small villages. In July 2021, an expectant mother of Kashipal village in Jashipur block of Mayurbhanj district on labour pain needed to be rushed to hospital. However, the ambulance could not reach the village due to lack of a motorable road, compelling family members to carry the woman on a cot to reach the ambulance waiting 2 km away from her house. The woman delivered a child on the way. In March 2021, women in Dumdumpada village under Rajgangpur block in Sundargarh district had to walk long distance to get water from a stream.

Sapalaguda, a small village in Mohana Tehsil in Gajapati district of Odisha is located 33 KM from district headquarters Paralakhemundi. The village had a population of 182. In 2001, Collector of the district reached the village on foot to enquire into the circumstances leading to death of three people. The family that fell victim to the tragedy had hosted guests and had used whatever rice they had and then had consumed fungus infested mango kernels as a last resort. The family lost three lives. Getting rice through PDS at the prescribed rate was impossible as the rice had to be carried on head or in cart for miles in the hilly terrain involving higher cost. If inhabitants chose to lift rice from the retailer at great distance, they had to walk miles, spend the night and carry rice back home.

A small village, say with thirty inhabitants, would make living of inhabitants highly vulnerable to adverse situations. Such a village would remain deficient in connectivity as well as basic amenities like drinking water, health workers, fair-price shops and primary education. That explains why unacceptable situations ranging from women walking miles to fetch water to an expectant mother being carried on a cot to a medical facility for delivery of child keep recurring. Such incidents could manifest even in developed districts as was the case in Nagada village in Jajpur district of Odisha.

A bridge over the Mahanadi over three kilometers

long connecting Cuttack with Nuapatna was completed a few years ago at a cost of Rs 157 crore. Another bridge over the Mahanadi, more than 3 kilometer long that connects Gopinathpur with Baideswar cost Rs 175 crore. Similar scale of investment would be needed to ensure connectivity to far flung small habitations, mostly in difficult terrain. Only improved road connectivity would not improve quality of life. Other amenities have to be provided for as well. Transformation of such tiny habitations, therefore, does not seem to be possible in near future.

We need to explore alternative approach. Odisha needs to embark upon a programme of consolidation of villages with the objective of relocating tiny villages and creating viable villages, each having a population of at least 500. Similarly, Odisha should have more Gram Panchayats so that a Panchayat should consist of up to three villages. Odisha should, perhaps, reduce the number of villages to around 35,000 and increase the number of Gram Panchayats to 15,000.

Dwindling Number of Odisha Candidates Getting into Civil Services

Civil Services Examination conducted by the UPSC through three stages — preliminary, main and interview — to select officers for the Indian Administrative Service (IAS), Indian Foreign Service (IFS), Indian Police Service (IPS) and Central Services perhaps continues to be the toughest and most keenly watched in the country.

How meticulously the examination has been designed and how only a few finally make it make a fascinating narrative. The preliminary examination consists of two papers of objective type (multiple choice) questions and carries a maximum of 400 marks. This stage serves as a screening test. Marks obtained by the candidates are not considered for determining their final order of merit. Merit is determined out of the total of 2,025 marks — written or main examination comprising seven papers of 1,750 marks while the interview carries a total of 275 marks.

In the previous examination held in October last year, a total of 10,40,060 candidates had applied for the examination, but 4,82,770 (46.41%) candidates appeared for it. Out of them, only 10,564 (2.2%) qualified for the main examination held in January. 2,053 (19.43%) of them qualified for the personality test (interview). Finally, 761 (37%) candidates were recommended for appointment.

These 761 candidates belonged to different categories- (i) General-263 (34.56%); (ii) EWS-86 (11.30%); (iii) OBC-229 (30.09%); (iv) SC-122 (16.03%) and (v) ST-61(8.01%). Out of the 761 candidates, 545 were males and 216, females (28.38%). Of the 761 candidates, 65.44%, numbering 498, belonged to EWS, OBC, SC & ST categories. For IAS, while 72 belonged to general category, 108 belonged to other categories and for IPS, out of 200 candidates recommended, 80 belonged to general category.

The fact that in the last examination, out of 482,770 candidates who took the preliminary examination, only 761 became successful (0.157%) through three stages of the examination process indicates how tough the examination is. The examination has its own compelling attraction for the brave, the determined and the passionate ones. It is not for persons having a casual interest in it.

UPSC discloses the cut off marks for each component of the examination for each category of candidates every year both for transparency and for the benefit of aspirants as this helps in preparation for examination. This year (2021) while the cut off mark for preliminary examination was 92.51 for general candidates, it was 68.71 for ST candidates. Similarly, for Main examination, cut off mark for general candidates was 736 and 682 for ST candidates. Overall cut off for general candidates was 944 and for ST candidates it was 876.

Many keep attempting to get in and sit for the examination a number of times subject to existing Rules that put a limit on the number of attempts and the age of the candidate. This year Shubham Kumar topped the examination with 52.04% marks scoring 1,054 marks — 878 in the written and 176 in the personality test. He was from engineering discipline and got into the Service in the third attempt. The next successful candidate, Jagrati Awasthi, scored 1052 marks – 859 in written papers and 193 in interview. She too was from engineering discipline and she got in, in her second attempt. The third rank holder, Ankita Jain, secured 1,051 marks — 839 in the main and 212 in the interview. She too was from engineering discipline and she had it in her fourth attempt. The fourth rank holder, Yash Jaluka, scored 1,046 marks (851 in written and 195 in interview). He was a student of Economics and cleared the examination in the first attempt. Incidentally, his parents now live in Barbil where he had studied in school for a few years.

The syllabus has been changing from time to time. To handle a huge number of applicants, screening has been introduced through preliminary examination. Profile of successful candidates has been changing. More and more students from Engineering and Management background are joining the civil services enriching the civil services.

In the past, candidates from Odisha had been performing reasonably well in the examination. However, performance of candidates from Odisha this year has been a matter of concern. Only nine seem to have been successful. In other words, only 1.18% of the successful 761 candidates belonged to Odisha. Better employment and business opportunities are stated to be reasons of lukewarm interest in civil services in some regions of the country. Gujarat is mentioned in this regard. On the other hand, upsurge of interest for a career in civil services has been noted in many states including Rajasthan and Bihar.

Job and business opportunities continue to be extremely limited in Odisha. A career in civil services is held in admiration in the state. It is therefore not correct to assume that Odisha youths are increasingly getting disinterested in civil services because of availability of better opportunities. The real reason seems to be the growing inadequacy in academic field that has made it increasingly difficult for Odisha candidates to compete.

Education sector in the state has been plagued with long spell of shortage of teaching staff that has affected quality of teaching. While students coming from the creamy layers of society have resources to get educated in reputed educational institutions outside the state, students from EWS, OBC, ST & SC segments have been badly affected with steady decline of teaching quality in local institutions. Performance of candidates belonging to these segments has been dismal.

The situation has become critical enough to warrant immediate measures by government. Persisting deficiencies in Colleges and State Universities need to be addressed to arrest further drift. Special coaching facilities have to be created in different zones for students aspiring to join the civil services. Financial help may have to be given to students of the EWS, OBC, SC & ST categories. Bihar has such a scheme for SC and ST persons who have cleared the preliminary examination.

❑

Some Thoughts on Padma Awards

Reportedly, Mamata Banerjee, Chief Minister of West Bengal, recently suggested awarding Bharat Ratna to India's mega star, Amitabh Bachchan. Suggestions for Ratan Tata for Bharat Ratna have also been aired in different forums.

While I would refrain from expressing who should be the choice for Bharat Ratna, I must say choosing process for Padma Awards still looks mysterious to me. I am aware that this land of ours is a land of exceptional talent and ability and it is a gargantuan task to select from thousands only a hundred or so for Padma Awards. Yet I have never been able to understand why the legendary Odia singer, Akshaya Mohanty, was denied the Award, why the indomitable, Shruti Mohapatra is yet to be honoured and why even the erudite nonagenarian Vedic scholar, Priyabrata Dash has not been selected for the Award.

Padma Vibhushan, the second highest civilian award of the Republic of India, is for exceptional and distinguished services. Since inception (till 2019), this honour has gone to about 300 individuals including 19 non-citizens and 12, posthumous. Subrahmanyan Chandrasekhar was the first to receive the award in 1968 from Science and Engineering discipline, in the 14th year of the institution of Padma Awards in 1954.

Persons honoured include 68 in Public Affairs, 57 in Arts, 53 in Civil Service, 40 in Literature and Education, 35 in Science and Engineering, 17 in Social Work, 13 in Medicine, 12 in Trade and Industry, 3 in Sports and 5 in other areas.

I have a feeling the process of selection for the honour needs a course correction to respond to Nation's growing shift to areas of technology while not ignoring the importance of dance, music, literature, public affairs and civil service etc.

P. N. Haksar was offered the Padma Vibhushan Award in 1973 for, among other services, his crucial diplomatic role in brokering the Indo-Soviet Treaty of Friendship and Cooperation and the Shimla Agreement. He declined the offer. He had said, "Accepting an award for work done somehow causes an inexplicable discomfort to me."

In the list of Padma Awardees of 2019, one finds Devrapalli Prakash Rao, the selfless Chaiwalla of Cuttack, who spent half of the earnings to educate children of slums. He had been honoured with Padma Shri. "Why was he not in the list of Padma Bhushans, like a former Bureaucrat?" I thought.

Another aspect of the Award that looks paradoxical is the present arrangement that allows the same person first a Padma Shri, then a Padma Bhushan and then a Padma Vibhushan.

How does one evaluate between two talented artists, say, Dipti Naval and Vidya Balan or between an Anupam Kher and a Kamal Hassan and decide on a Padma Award? Bhagat Singh and Aurobindo are not less venerable without such recognition nor are some Awardees even remembered.

That brings me to the issue of having a three-tier

Padma Awards. Perhaps it would be in consonance with the solemn resolve of ours, the people of India, to secure to all its citizens: EQUALITY of status and of opportunity, if we could do away with the present three-tier arrangement and settle for one, that is, Bharat Ratna. Should however it is not acceptable, we could have only Bharat Ratna and Padma Bhushan and do away with Shri and Vibhushan. .

In the speedometer of a car, one would see 0km/hour at one end and 200km/hour at the other end with 100km/hour in the middle. This configuration does not mean that one should drive at the maximum speed of 200 km per hour. For convenience, the preferred speed of 100 km/hour is put at the middle. What I am trying to explain is that the maximum speed indicted in the speedometer is not really meant to be achieved. The guidelines on Bharat Ratna mention about the maximum number of persons who may be honoured in a year and the number is 3. This number, I thought, was akin to the maximum speed of a speedometer.

In the final analysis, however, one wonders if the Padma awards are in sync with the democratic temper of the polity. Perhaps Morarji Desai, as Prime Minister, was right in doing away with the Awards.

❏

My Yoga Session with Swamiji

I too thought of joining the morning Yoga session in the city's Yoga Ashram. The Swami agreed to admit me. Strangely, the Swami even set apart an exclusive schedule for me when I would be his sole disciple. I agreed to the arrangement. In any case, I had no choice. On the first day he talked to me generally and mostly amiably. Perhaps he wanted me to feel comfortable with him and the environment of the Ashram. After half an hour or so, I felt a "feel good" ambience around. He then told me how other regulars had reacted when they got to know about my joining the Ashram class. "Many spoke bad about you while some spoke well", the Swami told me, with a smile.

This conflicting opinion about me, whom he had not seen nor heard of earlier, aroused a lot of interest in him, he said and he had an urge to see me. "I am here for your scrutiny," I said, with a smile. I passed through the preliminaries including Neti and then graduated soon to Surya Namaskar. Swamiji seemed satisfied with my progress. His body weight was surely much more than mine; but he loved doing Surya Namaskar with me. He believed practising Surya Namaskar was a sure way for acquiring physical prowess. One acquired the strength of an elephant through this yogic exercise, he told me. In his younger days he was very good at Surya Namaskar and at a stage he could even bend iron rods and break a window.

He then told me with a tinge of remorse in his tone how he got tainted with pride. As soon as he was aware of this blemish creeping in, he was wise enough to restrain himself and regained his composure and humility. As a penance, he is never again into the same state of elephantine pride mould. In a subtle way he had advised me to keep away from pride.

By then we had become friends. One day he told me how a few days back, he got up very early, around three in the morning and found himself in a state of melancholy. He took his harmonium to the Ashram temple; sang a prayer before Shivji, wept for some time and regained composure. It made an impact on me. One day I reminded him about how the regulars had reacted about me and asked him whether, after seeing me for a few months, he would go with the view of the majority. He smiled.

Then he said, "I remember a sweet Hindi film song. It said about the law of nature that turns every bright morning to a dark evening. In such a situation, small things like what we are and what names we bear are of no relevance. This is the world where even Devi Sita had got a bad name. That being the case, why should tears well up in our eyes on hearing what people say about us."

❑

Managing Minor Minerals in Odisha

Minor minerals in Odisha have emerged as an important source of government revenue. These comprise mostly stone, sand, murram, boulder and soil, and there are around 4000 "sources" in the state where these are amenable to mining. Despite slowdown of economy during the Covid pandemic, revenue collection from minor minerals in 2020-21 was Rs 962 crore, registering a growth of more than 40% over the previous year's collection of Rs 680 crore.

Management of these natural resources in Odisha had been with the Revenue Department and Minor minerals treated as Sairat sources. At the field level, these have been managed by the Tahsildar. With exponential increase in demand for these resources in development activities like construction of buildings, roads and bridges, exploitation of these resources has leapfrogged, posing challenges to the administrative infrastructure. Incidence of illegal exploitation has increased. Unscrupulous elements have taken law into their own hands and there are cases where officers discharging their duties have been victims of violence committed by such miscreants. It is public knowledge that huge pilferage goes on under political protection.

In view of the increasing inadequacies of the existing administrative arrangement, government decided to revamp the regulatory infrastructure so that the valuable natural resources were scientifically exploited. Besides meeting the economy's need for these minor minerals, the revamping is expected to yield higher revenue for the government.

Accordingly, management of minor minerals in Odisha has been transferred from Revenue and Disaster Management Department to Steel and Mines Department. Definition of Sairat (a subject allocated to Revenue and Disaster Management Department) in Rules of Business, has been modified excluding from it the minor minerals as defined under MMDR Act, 1957 to accommodate transfer of minor mineral management to Steel and Mines Department. Similarly, Directorate of Minor Minerals has been transferred from Revenue and DM Department to Steel and Mines Department. Mining Officer would be declared as Competent Authority and Deputy Director Mines, as Controlling Authority under OMMC Rules, 2016. For effective monitoring and supervision of sources, Directorate would have one Junior Mining Officer (JMO) in the field to supervise 30 sources, one Assistant Mining Officer (AMO) to supervise work of two JMOs, one Mining Officer (MO) to supervise work of 2 AMOs and 13 Deputy Director of Mining (DDM).

As per the new policy, government agencies would have priority for allocation of minor minerals sourced for timely completion of projects. Minor Minerals of high potential may, in consultation with Odisha Mining Corporation (OMC), be reserved for OMC.

It would be better if the JMO is stationed close to the source. This would ensure better supervision and control of the source. In the past, senior officers of the Directorate of Mining have been criminally prosecuted for complicity/ negligence in theft of minerals. Minor minerals too are equally, or, rather, more vulnerable to theft and since miscreants are extremely resourceful, it is most likely that theft would take place for Minor Minerals as well even under the revamped administrative arrangement. Territorial JMO, being on site and vulnerable to attacks by miscreants, should be free from enforcement job. He should process application, conduct auction, collect Royalty, and execute agreement with the lessee. Mining plan and agreement should also be under his purview. Vigilance wing should conduct surprise raids, catch stealing and impose fine.

A large number of officials have been proposed for the new Directorate. A very important and urgent task is to put the trained staff in place soon.

Another important issue relates to handing over and taking over of minor mineral sources. Such charge handing and taking over must not be a paper transaction. Authorised person of the Revenue Department must hand over assets to the competent Mining official on the field and clearly state how many and which are being worked legally and which are not.

Restructuring of the minor mineral administrative infrastructure is surely welcome and it is good that the need for adequate number of technical officials has been acknowledged. Right now, however, the situation remains confusing. Nothing much seems to have been done towards recruitment of officials. If precious time is lost in recruiting the staff, training them and deploying them in the field, huge damage would be done and large-scale pilferage would continue unabated for a long time.

❑

The Marginalised Poor

I told a friend recently that in case he wanted to see the common man's determination to live, he could spend a few hours, incognito, in the chamber of a well-known Oncologist in the Acharya Harihar Regional Cancer Centre at Cuttack and see how the young, the middle aged and elderly ones, afflicted with the fearful disease, would be patiently listening to the doctor; wait for the prescription to be handed over to them and take leave of the doctor with gratitude and a smile. I had watched this scene one day for hours and never did I notice fear or anxiety in the face of any patient. Hope was writ large on each face. That was the message I received that day; the message that the Aam Admi wants to survive; he wants to surmount challenges howsoever daunting the task may be. It however looked strange to me that while the political system we are in draws its power from the people most of whom are poor, yet in the day-to-day life we all realise that the prevailing mindset tilted in favour of the affluent class.

The other day, most of the important streets and markets of Bhubaneswar displayed fruits in good quantity. Fruits were in great demand for a very important occasion; Sabitri Brata, when the wife prayed for the long life of the husband; she is on fast and breaks fast with some fruits. She worshipped Sabitri, the epitome of strength, valor, chastity and integrity. She puts on a new sari. Shops do

81

brisk business. Prices reach dizzy heights. Behind such exuberance, however, there exists a zone of silence, where the poor lives. That is the zone where many families do not have the resources to buy a sari or the fruits. Such harsh reality showed itself just on the eve of the Sabitri Brata in a year in the suburb of Bhubaneswar when the young wife of a carpenter took her life following the inability of her husband to buy her a sari for the occasion. Most likely the husband was finding his meagre income too inadequate even to service the debt of the family. The news was cruel enough to disturb one's conscience. The picture of a young housewife hanging dead leaving behind a two-year-old crying child while the husband was away haunted me for quite some time; even while I robbed shoulders with the buyers in the crowded daily market of Bhubaneswar to buy a few things for my wife to observe the Brata the next day. Nor could I respond with adequate warmth to our daughter's delight who called from Naperville to let us know that for Sabitri Brata she was able to get six pieces of bangles for three dollars from a local shop. There was yet another gruesome death when an old couple, unable to bear the pangs of poverty, decided to end lives in Ganjam District. The man and wife consumed poison. They had left a written note stating that they had been deprived of essential facilities like a house under the Indira Awas Yojana and a ration card. One of them died and the other was taken to the hospital in a serious condition. Acute poverty and abject deprivation manifest in such tragic incidents in our society where one unfortunately witnesses indulgence of the rich.

Though the poor exhibits great determination to live, he suffers a life of great turbulence. Sometimes it looks as if the society has lost its sensitivity to the issues of deprivation and sufferings of fellow countrymen. It seems it has become insane and looks the other way when calamity of the type described here strikes poor families. Is it because we have lost the basic human trait to respect human life? Ours is the country where the maximum number of babies are born in a day—as many as seventy thousand, out of 3,53,000 babies born in a day the world over. This profuse production perhaps generates a feeling of complacency and laxity towards human life and we tend to be indifferent and do not invest in our human resource the way we should.

Had Orissa been a separate country, it could have been in the list of thirty five most populous countries of the world. Countries like Canada, Romania, Australia, Netherlands, Malaysia, Sri Lanka and Venezuela have less population than Orissa. Let us have a close look at the annual personal consumption expenditure in Constant 2005 International Dollars ($) for three of these countries. In case of Canada, personal consumption was $15,094 of which Health accounted for 575 dollars; Housing 5613 dollars; Food 2271 dollars; Clothing 823 dollars; Education 387 dollars and Transport 2886 dollars. For Australia, personal consumption was $14036; Food accounted for $2429; Health $724; Clothing $557; Housing $4240. For Netherlands, total personal consumption was$13282; Food accounted for $2299; Clothing $904; Health $474. In case of China, the total personal consumption was $2292 of which Health accounted for $159; Housing $440; Food $932; Clothing $63.

In case of India one gets details of the household expenditure from the survey made by the government from time to time. A sample of 31,673 rural households and 18,624 urban households spread over the entire country was surveyed in the Consumer Expenditure Survey of the 64th round of NSS, carried out in 2007-08. It revealed that the Average Monthly Per Capita Consumer Expenditure (MPCE) in 2007-08 was Rs.559 in rural Odisha and Rs.1438 in urban Odisha at 2007-08 prices. In rural household in Odisha, the per capita expenditure on pan, tobacco and intoxicant comes to Rs 13.48 and on beverage etc. Rs37.80 making a total of Rs51.28—much more than the man spent on milk and milk products which account for only Rs10.50. In urban Odisha, expenditure on pan, tobacco, intoxicants and beverages etc. comes to Rs 142.17 with beverages etc. accounting for Rs125.97. A person on the other hand spends only Rs57.34 on milk and milk products. On cereals, a person in rural Odisha spent Rs136.57 out of his total monthly expenditure of Rs.558.95. He spent Rs37.29 on clothing; and Rs 11.87 on education. On an average, a person in rural Odisha consumed 13.13 kg rice in a month. If he had a ration card and did receive the cheap rice, then he would have spent Rs 26.26 on rice. If he had no ration card as the old man in Ganjam who consumed poison in desperation, he would have spent around Rs 150 to get the rice and his wife would also have needed a similar amount. Since they could have not afforded this expenditure they preferred to die. This is not an ideal story in a welfare state.

Analysis of the per capita expenditure indicates a depressing scenario. The rich human resource of the state needs to be guided to improve quality of the life. In Canada the number of babies born per day is around 1000 whereas in Odisha around 2300 babies are born per day. Sadly, Odisha continues to be home to a large number of poor people. We must have a more meaningful approach to governance to prevent recurrence of traumatic manifestation of deprivation. It is certainly possible for a Block Development Officer to visit each household in a Block. He needs to do that and he must spend quality time with each family. If a householder does not have a ration card, the BDO should have the authority to issue one on the spot. The old couple who preferred poison could have had a meaningful life with a ration card. The countries I have referred to have smaller populations than ours. Yet the countries have progressed well. We also can, provided we face the prevailing problems with far sight and dedication. We should not promote further marginalisation of the poor. It would be an act of cruelty to stifle his potential through mal governance.

❏

Entry of Spoils System
in Odisha Bureaucracy

It was as early as 1858 when India adopted a permanent civil service appointed through competitive examination. UK adopted a similar system twelve years later and USA opted for such a system only twenty-five years later. USA had been manning government posts by people picked up as political patronage. The pernicious system, known as Spoils System, started during the administration of President Andrew Jackson in 1829 and continued till it was abolished by a law known as the Pendleton Act in 1883. The merit system of recruitment commenced in India since 1858, and continued after India attained independence in 1947. Indian Civil Service (ICS) was considered one of the finest public services of the world and it became a model for other countries. The system insulated recruitments from political patronage and ensured neutrality of the civil service - so essential in a pluralistic society and a polity that has opted for a parliamentary democracy and a multi-party system. Spoils system was never the preferred option in India for manning government posts.

It is relevant to recall Odisha Chief Minister's stand on contractual appointments. On October 14, 2022, Chief Minister said to the media, "I am delighted to announce that the State Cabinet has decided to abolish the contractual system of recruitment permanently – the era of contractual recruitment has come to an end. The Chief Minister further said, "In 2000, with the blessings of all of you I got an opportunity to serve Mother Odisha. The post-Super Cyclone situation and the fragile financial conditions then were biggest challenges for me. It was indeed a black period for the Odisha economy. The state exchequer was empty. There was tremendous pressure on our economy. We were lagging behind in various fields including health, education, infrastructure, agriculture, irrigation and many others. Our priority then was to bring improvement in all these sectors within our limited resources," he added, "Under the circumstances, the government was forced to abolish regular posts. It was a difficult decision and very painful for me. The youths of my state were running from pillar to post for employment. The only thing that was on top of my mind was – when would the situation improve? When would our children get regular recruitment in state government? Now our economy has improved significantly. Odisha has created a new identity for itself in the field of development in the country."

Against this backdrop, one needs to view the sudden and unexpected appointment by Government of Odisha of Manoj Kumar Mishra as Principal Secretary to Government, Electronics and Information Technology on contractual basis. The decision is important and merits a discussion. The General Administration Department Notification dated the 29th of December, 2022 while appointing him as such, stated that Mishra's resignation from the Indian Railway Traffic Service (IRTS) had been accepted on the 28th December by the Ministry of Railways. It also said Mishra would remain in additional charge of Special Secretary to Government (Rail Coordination), Commerce and Transport Department.

He shall be entitled to consolidated remuneration as is paid (Pay plus DA) to the officer of equivalent rank and shall be provided with the required facilities for smooth discharge of his official duties.

Let us have a look at the office memorandum of GA and PG Department of Government of Odisha bearing number GAD-SC-GCS-0169-2020 10682/Gen., dated 19th of April, 2022 on regularisation of qualified workers appointed against sanctioned posts. The office memorandum has flagged a few very important issues on the matter of recruitment for government posts. These include the following:

(i) Equality of opportunity is the hallmark for public employment and it is in terms of the Constitutional scheme only.

(ii) The filling of vacancies cannot be done in a haphazard manner or based on patronage or other considerations.

(iii) The state is meant to be a model employer and can make appointments only in accordance with the rules framed under Article 309 of the Constitution.

(iv) Regularisation is not and cannot be a mode of recruitment by any State within the meaning of Article 12 of the Constitution of India.

(v) Any regular appointment made on a post under the State or Union without issuing advertisement inviting applications from eligible candidates and without holding a proper selection where ail eligible candidates get a fair chance to compete, would violate the guarantee enshrined under Article 16 of the Constitution.

(vi) If it is a contractual appointment, the appointment comes to an end at the end of the contract.

Orissa Government Rules of Business which have been framed by the Governor in exercise of powers conferred by Clause (3) of Article 166 of the Constitution of India states that (i) each Department of the Secretariat shall consist of a Secretary to Government who shall be the official head of that department.(ii) "Secretary" means a Secretary to the Government of Orissa and includes a Principal Secretary, a Special Secretary, an Additional Secretary, a Joint Secretary, a Deputy Secretary and an Under Secretary.

In the case under discussion, a person, not in any government service, has been picked up by the Government and appointed as Principal Secretary in one Department and Special Secretary in another Department. These two departments do not have any functional similarity nor do these departments need similar or same domain expertise. The person selected does not seem to be specially equipped to do justice to both the assignments. Why he was picked up from the market in a secretive manner without an open advertisement that would have elicited response from people having better domain expertise and practical experience, is not known. Why one department of Government has been placed in charge of an outsider deviating from the normal practice of posting a suitable officer from the IAS cadre is also not clear and seems to be in conflict with the IAS Cadre Rule.

It could be argued that the selected person while on deputation from the IRTS with the state government did function as Special Secretary, Commerce and Transport Department and Commissioner, Rail Coordination and also as Secretary, Electronics and Information Technology. This, however, cannot be a ground for picking him up from market and putting him in charge of these posts. Odisha's performance in handing over land for critical railway projects has been highly unsatisfactory. In software sector the state continues to remain a poor player, exports of software sector in last three years have reached a plateau. Odisha is yet to adopt RTI Online. E Despatch arrangement is yet to become robust and sustainable.

In the Schedule of Posts in the Odisha IAS cadre, there are nine posts of Principal Secretary. Equivalent number of IAS officers is also in position in ex-cadre posts. Two IAS officers of 1998 batch of IAS were posted as Principal Secretary only recently. An officer of 1999 Batch of IRTS could be in the grade equivalent to Principal Secretary in state Government only after many years. Here is however a case where the person has been appointed as Principal Secretary even when there was no such vacancy. The contractual appointment also seems open ended. The procedure followed is in stark violation of the norms stipulated in GA Department's Memorandum referred to above and also the Chief Minister's public stand on contractual appointment.

Government decision in this case looks inexplicable; it violates the time tested merit system in recruitment for government posts prevalent in the country and is a clear endorsement of Spoils System that could have far reaching consequences and compromise political neutrality of state's bureaucracy. There are strong reasons for Government to set things right by nullifying the decision. If that does not happen, Government of India needs to look at the issue and issue appropriate advisory. If that also does not happen, we perhaps have to learn to live both with a partisan bureaucracy and compromising transparency in recruitment.

My Friend Talked about the Magic of Indrajav

My friend Gopal's younger son worked in Thomson Reuters and the daughter-in-law, in Dell. She got transferred to Austin and the family shifted there. Gopal's son is now looking for a job there. Talking about his son this morning, Gopal turned nostalgic.

This son of his was a very healthy child when he was about four months old. Suddenly he had an attack of a virulent type of diarrhea that did not respond to medical treatment Gopal could have access to. He tried his best to save the child. A pediatrician of repute, working in a Medical College, was contacted. He responded and assured recovery. He would, however, take ten thousand rupees. It was a big amount for the government servant in 1975. Gopal agreed, but with a condition. The specialist doctor would be paid transport cost and normal fee but would be given the big amount only if the infant was cured. To prove his credibility, Gopal handed over the amount in his presence, to a common friend. The Doctor agreed and the infant received his attention and medicine. The diarrhea, however, didn't subside. Gopal lost hope.

A kindly peon working in his office who lived in the neighbouring village saw the plight of the family. He suggested use of Indrajava. "What is that", distraught Gopal asked Bohidar, the peon. It is the seed of a creeper called Korei. "Where do I get it"? Gopal asked. "From the local trader, Ganesh Narayan, who has been sending wagons of Indrajava to Mumbai" he said. Gopal contacted the trader. "How many Bags do you need Sir?" the kindly Kediaji asked the tax officer, Gopal. "Kediaji", Gopal said, "my infant son is fighting for his life. I am told Indrajav could save him. A small quantity would be enough". Kediaji promptly sent about a kilogram of the seed. Bohidar taught the way the seed had to be soaked in warm water overnight and then the milk from the seed taken out, dried, pulverised and how a very small quantity of the powder would have to be given orally to the child at six hourly interval. The infant had only two doses and got fully cured.

Gopal then told me about his office assistant who went to his home town, about a hundred kilometers away, and stayed on. Office work suffered and Gopal looked for him in desperation." I am fighting for my life here at home in Bargarh, the office assistant said, "I am having diarrhea that doesn't respond to medicines I am taking". This happened sometime after Gopal's son was cured Gopal sent to him in an envelope some Indrajav seeds with a note explaining how he would use it. The office assistant got cured after a day and reported to duty.

"You must have noticed Korei creeper, widely growing in the wild along the road between Keonjhar and Rourkela", Gopal told me. "The creeper has white flowers" he told. "Indrajav is available in Baidya Store in old Bhubaneswar as well" he said.

❑

Remembering a Teacher

One of my nephews studied in Biswambar Bidyapitha at Puri. His father had come to Puri on transfer from Koraput and wanted his son to study in this particular school. The headmaster would not agree. He was not sure that a student, coming from a modest school in distant Koraput, a small town, could ever bring glory to the school. "Go to Zila School", he advised the student. "You have a transfer certificate, your father, a senior government servant, has come here on transfer. They in Zila School would take you to their roll without any difficulty," he said. The boy was at a loss. His father did not agree. He was insistent that his son would study only in Biswambar Bidyapaith. The headmaster ultimately relented and agreed to assess the boy a little closely. The boy passed his scrutiny and joined the school. The headmaster was the renowned Padmanabh Dash.

Yesterday (4th July, 2013) that boy, Sudhansu Sekhar Dash, who had passed his Matriculation in 1979 met an elderly relation, Shyama Sundar Mahapatra, in Puri in a function. The elderly gentleman was for some time teaching in the School before he joined a public sector undertaking. The boy is now grown up. He is a senior Executive in a Bank and is living in Bangalore. He recollected how his Headmaster was closely monitoring his progress in the school. He even had scrutinised his answer sheets in both papers in Mathematics in the Matriculation Examination as soon as the Examination was over and congratulated him saying that he would score 100% in each paper. He actually scored 100 in one and 99 in the other paper. By recounting this experience, Sudhansu was paying his respects to his venerable teacher who is no more.

They talked more about the old School. It was now the turn of Mr. Mahapatra. He remembered the celebrated Padmanabh Dash. After the half yearly examination every year, the Headmaster would sell the Answer sheets as waste paper and the sale proceeds would be used for meeting sundry expenses of the school. No one knew what used to be done about the Annual Examination Answer sheets. When Government decided to take over the School from private management, the Headmaster divulged a secret before his colleagues. He had saved a lakh of rupees by selling the Answer sheets of the Annual Examinations of each class over years. The money was in a Bank. He did not want to hand over the handsome amount to the government. He discussed various alternatives and before the School was converted to a Government High School, he spent the entire money buying costly but necessary equipment for the Science Laboratories of the School so that the students would have the benefit of well-equipped laboratories. He knew too well that in the system of working in the government, the hundred thousand rupees he had painstakingly saved by selling old Answer sheets over years, could not have been utilised in that very school. The money would have lost its special identity being a part of government money. And it would have taken years for the School to have modern equipment for its laboratories.

This in brief was how both Sudhansu and Mr.

Mahapatra remembered a great Teacher, yesterday for quite some time, in his absence. This is how a great teacher is remembered. He lives in many hearts and there he lives long.

❏

Defining a Teacher

Today I remember a Teacher and I am writing from my experience as a Teacher. When I was doing my Honours in Ravenshaw College, Prof Shriram Chandra Dash once had asked a very bright student of our class to speak on what he understood about Sovereignty. It was a big class, in the huge Chemistry Lecture Theatre of the College. The student started brilliantly and very lucidly spoke how various political philosophers including John Austin had defined Sovereignty. Dr Dash was getting impatient and finally lost his cool when the student went on quoting wise men. In his usual style he took the student to task and said, "I learnt from you what others said about Sovereignty; but what I wanted to hear from you, in your own words, is what you have understood about it." I learnt what learning is about. Essence of learning is the ability to understand and express on a matter/ issue in your own way.

I joined as a Lecturer to teach Political Science to the Post Graduate students of Utkal University. I was in this assignment for just one academic year before joining the IAS. Post Graduate Department of Political Science had 128 students in each batch. I became aware that many students viewed a teacher as role model and loved to follow in his footsteps. Thereby they received good amount of motivation. Even today, a teacher should be a role model even though to be so, he has to compete with film actors and cricket players.

I realised I was not equipped to make equal impact on all 128 students through my teachings but it would be a reasonable performance if half of them could be on my wave length while I taught and the rest not very much away from it. A successful teacher, I was convinced, enhanced the inquisitiveness of the students and set the students on quest. A teacher enabled and empowered a student to be on auto pilot mode.

❏

Relationship

Isaw the young friend this morning by the side of the Vivekananda Marg, in front of the Hanuman Temple. He was saying his prayer. He smiled as soon as our eyes met. I was returning home and he was to go to the Temple garden nearby. We walked together, towards our destinations. He has been regularly following me in social media, he said. I smiled. I find in him a person ever eager to take up good causes--- helping persons in need; coming forward to participate in cleaning the temple premises, taking a sick man to the hospital, attending funerals of people not even close to him.

This morning he came up with a different issue. He told me about his mother-in-law. The lady is obese and has been suffering from various ailments as well. She used to go on walk with her husband regularly till a fateful day. She could not keep pace with him and at one stage she presumed he was still at some distance and she would be able to reach him. She walked on till she thought it appropriate to give up and she returned home. On return, she found him at home.

From that day not only did she stop accompanying him on walk but stopped walking on her own as well and fell victim to greater obesity and many ailments. My young friend then spoke about his efforts to motivate his wife to accompany him on walk. He feels his wife was adding weight and must have regular exercise. She, however, feels that her child was too small to be left alone. She promises to accompany him after the child grows up.

I could not decide whether his mother-in-law was wrong or her husband. But I remembered an incident about another couple. Both were professionals. The man was driving the scooter and the lady was at the back. The scooter negotiated a road hump and the lady fell off. The driver, unmindful of the incident, moved on quite a distance till the silence at the back became loud enough. He drove back on the look out of the missing wife and found her with a few bruises and justifiable anger. Both being doctors, they went to the hospital where they worked. We soon came to know about this. After a few days, both visited us and the lady narrated her experience. Her husband was apologetic and pleaded guilty. We realised that the rancor had worn out. Their love for each other had made them forget the incident. I did not mention about this incident to my young friend this morning. But we did talk for some time about relationship.

"In a family the male member, I said, was more responsible to make relationship succeed. He has to be the leader in sacrifice, making adjustments, in counseling, in meeting crises. He has to be the ultimate dispenser of comfort, security and justice. The young man was not sure if I was correct. "In many families, the husband felt he was immortal. He would not write a will; he will keep financial secrets close to his chest; he would not disclose how much he is in debt and who the lenders are; nor will he say where he has sunk his money and how much has been given on loan and to whom. Suddenly death strikes and the lady finds herself totally helpless. This is pure and simple tyranny," I said.

I found him still unconvinced. "In many cases, the lady does not appreciate if the husband has helped someone needy even if the help was rendered to a person who was a blood relation. This attitude puts relationship on strain", he said. "In such a case also, I would blame the husband, I said. He should have taken the wife into confidence. He should have explained to her the circumstances of the case and even should have suggested that she should take a decision in the matter. Family is not about perennial domination of either the husband or the wife; nor is it about permanent serfdom of either. It is an institution where there is no single cook. Here both must cook. And I would blame the man if the marriage is under strain", I said.

He still remained unconvinced. I smiled. "I don't want you to agree, I want you to think", I said. He was somewhat relieved and smiled. We parted company. He went towards the garden and I walked home.

❑

Air Connection from Bhubaneswar to Dubai, Singapore and Bangkok

Odisha Chief Minister while addressing the Odia diaspora in Dubai on June 29, 2022, had indicated about early operation of direct flights between Bhubaneswar and Dubai. That Odisha Government had been going ahead with a viability gap funding (VGF) plan for an air link between the two cities was indicated by Government officials present during the Dubai visit of the Chief Minister. VGF is a government grant arrangement to support infrastructure projects that are economically justified but fall short of financial viability.

Chief Secretary who had accompanied the Chief Minister had clarified that government would subsidise airlines willing to operate direct flights between the two cities. It is believed that government would provide subsidy to flight operators for a limited period of time and expect that the operations would be financially viable within that period. Such an arrangement had been taken recourse to not long ago, for flights to and from Kuala Lumpur and Bangkok. The experiment failed. Benefit to the economy from this expensive experiment was little. Footfall of foreign tourists on Odisha soil remained negligible. With this experience, what prompted government to repeat the VGF model for Dubai connection is not clear.

It seems almost everyone in Odisha, including even those who do not intend flying abroad, is now happy with the recent Cabinet decision on Bhubaneswar getting air connectivity with Dubai, Bangkok and Singapore. It seems Government had invited bids form operators and received only one offer. Why the Government accepted the single offer is not clear. Details like when the good day would arrive and flights to Dubai, Bangkok and Singapore will commence; frequency of these flights, timings of arrival and departure are still not disclosed. Nor are fares indicated. Not a word has been said about who would fix the fare if all of it would be deposited with the government. What the operating cost would be is not known either. Press report indicated that Government would pay the operator the operating cost. Present moment, it seems, is for clapping and rejoicing.

In the absence of these details, one cannot make accurate assessment about the likely cost of this announcement to the taxpayers. Even then, an attempt has been made to make a rough estimate of the likely cost. These sectors have not looked economically viable to established operators. Otherwise, Bhubaneswar would have been having direct links with the three international gateways, or at least one or two of them. Apart from India's mega cities like Mumbai, Delhi, Chennai, Hyderabad, Kolkata, Bangalore and Ahmadabad having adequate number of direct flights to Dubai, many other cities like Amritsar, Chandigarh, Lucknow and Nagpur besides a few cities of Kerala too have direct air connection to Dubai. In case of Singapore, besides the mega cities, Vishakhapatnam and Madurai have direct flights. Lucknow has a direct flight to Bangkok.

As things stand now, the passenger-load for the three

cities from and to Bhubaneswar would be modest. Flights to Kuala Lumpur and Bangkok from Bhubaneswar in the past indicated low passenger load. While Dubai-Bhubaneswar sector could show somewhat higher passenger load, it could be much below 70 per cent. Singapore and Bangkok would offer much lower occupancy. In this analysis, it has been assumed that 70 per cent passenger load in Bhubaneswar flights to/ from Dubai, Singapore and Bangkok would ensure a break-even operation and the average occupancy for the three routes would be only 40 per cent. The average fare for these sectors has been assumed at Rs 20,000. On this basis, one up and down flight at 40 per cent occupancy for all the three sectors in a 186 seater aircraft would need a support for about Rs 65 lakh. 100-day flights per year (twice a week flight) would cost Rs 65 crore.

In the instant case, how long the proposed viability gap funding arrangement would continue is not known. The single offer has reportedly been accepted. Whether the offer binds the government in an open-ended arrangement is not known either. The rough cost estimate indicated above is an indicative figure. Actual cost could be even higher. What advantages would flow from this arrangement are not clear. The cost benefit ratio of the proposed investment needs to be placed in the public domain.

❑

Swachh Bharat Mission in Bhubaneswar

Swachh Bharat Mission was launched by Government of India on the 2nd of October, 2014 with focus on having open defecation free (ODF) towns and scientific solid waste management in urban centres. However, Odisha's capital city Bhubaneswar continues to grapple with the problems, particularly the solid waste management.

The city generates approximately 520 tons of Municipal Solid Waste per day. Three private contractors in 57 wards and the Municipal Corporation directly in rest of the 10 wards, do the door-to-door garbage collection, street sweeping, Municipal Solid Waste (MSW) transportation, drain cleaning, drain de-silting, conservancy cleaning and bush cutting. These activities are done every day to ensure city's cleanliness, and keep it garbage-free and hygienic. NGO assistance has been availed for motivating households to ensure segregation of solid wastes. Road sweeping is carried twice a day in commercial areas. Night sweeping of main roads is done through mechanical sweeping. MSW collected from various parts of the city is transported to Temporary Transfer Station (TTS)- an area of about 26 acres near Sainik School. Waste collected there is transported to the dump site – an area of over 61 acres- at Bhuasuni, where the wastes are dumped and levelled in layers. There is no operational solid waste treatment plant in Bhubaneswar as yet. Currently, 65 vehicles engaged in MSW management are being tracked and monitored under PPP mode.

By now, about ten micro composting centres (MCCs) have been established to process wastes to organic manure under 'Mo Khata' initiative. Plan is to have about 43 such facilities in the city. Some quantities of organic manure are now being sold and this welcome initiative holds out great potential. City dwellers should make use of this modest but people friendly initiative.

BMC has made available adequate number of 120-240 litre bins for collection of garbage. The bins, however, present an ugly sight. There is always more garbage strewn around each of them and the spot hosts stray cattle and dogs who make the place messy. Though BMC plans to do away with bins and ensure door-to-door collection, large number of squalor loving denizens however thinks and act differently and make a habit of throwing garbage on the lane after the pickup vehicle has left the area. Throwing garbage on the lanes is a day-long activity. For strange reasons, BMC has been displaying undue tolerance to this irresponsible behaviour. Need of the hour is to identify some ugly spots where this habit is strong, fix CCTV cameras, capture images of people in flagrante delicto and initiate criminal action.

The city's garbage disposal arrangement was disrupted recently when movement of vehicles to dumping yard was obstructed by some people. Sometimes the scavengers could have issues over payment of wage as well. Such contingencies need to be avoided through better planning and having alternatives.

Unless there is overwhelming support and

participation of city dwellers and commercial establishments in door-to-door delivery of garbage, efforts made so far by Bhubaneswar civic body would remain baby steps and the goal of having a garbage-free city with satisfactory MSW management will be a daunting task.

Indore city is widely acclaimed as one of the cleanest and recently the Mayor of Bhubaneswar paid a visit to the city to have a personal experience of the Indore model. Some best practices of the city need mention. Indore city that generates over 1,115 MT of garbage a day gets all of it collected from the source whether it is a household or commercial establishment. The door-to-door service was started in January 2016 as a pilot project in two of the 84 wards in the city. It took about a year to achieve 100% door-to-door garbage collection. Indore also achieved segregation of waste at source at 100% of its households and commercial units. Domestic hazardous waste in Indore is sent straight to the Central Domestic Hazardous Waste Treatment Facility to be incinerated.

The way waste generated in a huge Mandi in Indore was handled is worth taking note of. Choithram Mandi, the largest in Central India, generates about 20-25 MTPD fruit and vegetable waste. Municipal Corporation of Indore opted for decentralized processing of organic waste and established the Bio-CNG Plant of 20 MTPD in December 2017 at a cost of Rs,15 crore. About 800 kg of purified and compressed Bio CNG having 95% pure Methane gas generated every day is used to operate about 15 city buses. Indore city makes use of Modular toilets in places where slums have been developed on private land, disputed land and transit settlements where constructing permanent toilet complexes is not feasible.

Wholesome participation of the citizenry in the cleaning drive, restraint on waste generating propensity, adoption of technology, having multiple dumping sites, temporary transfer station, enforcing law against people throwing garbage indiscriminately are some of the key areas that need to be addressed to make Swachh Bharat Mission a success in Bhubaneswar city.

❏

Remembering a Friend

Sribatsa Nanda was a classmate of mine in Ravenshaw College while we were studying Science in the Intermediate stage His command over Mathematics was awesome. He was never the type of students who would slog for hours over books. He was jovial by nature, liked to joke with friends and would wear a look of being non-serious in studies. Results in examination would show otherwise. He would excel in all subjects. Occasionally I would see him in the Common Room of the East Hotel-- where we stayed--- alone, reading a newspaper or, in company, enjoying a cricket commentary in the radio. He was one of the few who loved to wear a Dhoti and was quite comfortable and proud of his sartorial preference. He could have joined any discipline of knowledge and even could have easily taken up any prestigious job in government sector. But he had his vision set. And he took to teaching as his career. He was a respected teacher in the Regional Engineering College at Rourkela. On superannuation, he joined a private College and continued to teach. Teaching was his passion.

We met accidentally one day in the morning on the road, near our house. We were meeting after years. We talked for a while and he remembered my father. His fondness and admiration for him moved me a bit and I told him about an incident relating to my father. On retirement from civil service, my father kept himself busy in many activities, mostly in the areas of social and economic mobilisation of the deprived segments of the society. He also spent some time in developing a good school in the area we lived. The school grew big and BJB English Medium School is now one of the most sought after schools in the city, He used to teach a few blind students of the BJB College residing in the Hostel nearby. I never knew about this passion of my father while he was alive. After his demise, a close associate of his had told us of his pastime.

One evening, his teaching schedule got upset as my father overstayed in another programme. He suddenly remembered his promise to teach the blind students for some time that evening. It was examination time. He hurried to reach them while regretting the delay. His friend and he finally reached the Hostel. It was late but he kept the promise. By then the students had switched off the light and were on the beds in the protection of mosquito nets. My father entered the room with his usual endearingly loud voice asking them to get up. The children immediately came out of the beds; switched on the light. Father taught them for over an hour and left them only after getting an assurance that they would have no problem answering questions in the examination the next day.

Sribatsa was listening with rapt attention like a child. I saw tears welling up and rolling down. I saw a sensitive Teacher in him weeping. We spent some more time and then I returned home and he went to the place where he was staying. That was the last that I saw him. One day I heard about his sudden passing away. It was my turn to shed tears in memory of a good friend.

❑

Hurried Facelift Operations in Bhubaneswar

The other day, flurry of activities were noticed on some lanes in Bhubaneswar. Hurried cleaning was done, heavy machineries on city's selected roads rolled giving a fresh layer of black coat to them and denizens wondered if the VVIP would be passing that way. President of India was visiting the city and that made the authorities work in a hurry.

Such occasions when VVIPs visit a place, make many people happy, for good reasons. Renovation works are taken up on urgency and often with huge costs. On such occasions, normal financial prudence is thrown to the winds. The focus is on optics and the system relapses to state of indifference once the big event is over. Bhubaneswar now hosts the Hockey World Cup - a mega event, and citizens are experiencing a massive facelift and attendant extravagance.

Let us have a quick look at the smart city infrastructure's dark underbelly. A wide road in front of the BJB Junior College Building was extensively renovated; a culvert was constructed to facilitate flow of storm water. All these were done not long ago. Suddenly a loaded truck negotiating the culvert fell into the drain when a few concrete slabs of the culvert gave way. Now the entire drain has been filled with earth and perhaps there won't be any culvert. How the storm water would be regulated is not clear. In the meantime, the wide road was badly damaged. Road and culvert maintenance jobs, by and large, suffer from quality deficit and public discontent and disillusionment keep swelling. The road in the meantime has been repaired and looks healthy. No one knows how long the shine would last.

City roads keep being dug up for many reasons that include laying cables, attending to choked sewer, raising welcome arches for political leaders, erecting makeshift stage for music show. Footpaths are by and large under occupation by vendors; and where these are not, are unsuitable for pedestrians. There are non-functional e-toilets, non-functional e-kiosks. Execution of works continues to be unprofessional and clumsy.

Concrete works are hardly moist cured which is a common method that ensures concrete slab becomes strong and durable. The way profligacy is resorted to by multiple agencies for projects with little consideration towards quality indicates total absence of accountability and, consequently, millions of rupees of public money get wasted. We soon experience potholes on roads, water-logging, spillage of sewage, outbreak of Dengue.

Discipline and accountability would have ensured a much better urban infrastructure and value for money. It could avoid facelift measures and hurried applying of veneer. Window-dressing culture, however, is now too deep-rooted to be dispensed with. Its virtues are many. It generates a feel-good ambience, it keeps primary stakeholders happy. The contractors, the suppliers and the supervisors make windfall gains. The segments that feel shortchanged are the non-corporate taxpayers and the citizens. In any case, the prevailing style of governance has ensured steady diminution of these two segments and window dressing is a part of that culture.

❑

Sribatsa --- the Miracle Linesman

Sribatsa has been an epitome of professionalism and integrity. I had been seeing him in our part of the city since we moved to our house some years ago.

I saw him on a hot day in May, scanning innumerable mysterious switches inside a box fixed to a telephone pole near the college playground; sometimes I saw him negotiating an improvised ladder to reach a defect in the overhead telephone lines near our house. He would visit our house and, knowing where our fixed telephone had been placed, would walk up to it and examine the heavy instrument, to listen to the bizarre sounds coming out of the receiver. He would then connect his grotesque looking handphone to our telephone and speak to some unseen person. Then our phone would suddenly spring back to life, after having been dead for three days.

I always considered him a "miracle man" and respected him. He too has been always courteous and reverential towards me. In spite of our bonding, he would never listen to me if I told him, during a chance meeting on the road, about malfunctioning of my telephone. He sprang to action only after a complaint had been communicated to him by his office through his telephone.

He sounded somewhat melancholic while he told me,

a month ago, about his impending retirement. He knew this news would upset me.

One morning I saw him on a culvert near the local telephone exchange. He wished me. I stopped walking and preferred to talk to him while waiting for my friend. I was anxious to know how he would spend time on retirement after a few days. He had been avoiding answering this question earlier. This morning, however, he opened his mind. Maybe by now he had decided on what he would do.

He will be engaged in mushroom and poultry farming and help his son to grow in this business. He had bought adequate land, not far from our city and would start his venture soon. He looked both confident and contented.

"Why did you not go back home in the evening but preferred to sleep in the Telephone Exchange?" I asked. His reply only confirmed my faith in this person-- a man of integrity and professionalism. The recent road digging in the area had affected many telephones in the Court complex nearby and he had been asked to complete the rectification job quickly. He worked late into last night and did not like to return home, miles away, on his bicycle.

He slept inside the Telephone Exchange, his Temple, for decades, the door of which may not open for him for a night's shelter, once he walked into retirement after a few days.

❏

Ahimsa in the Preamble
of our Constitution

A mind free from violence in any form reveals compassion for all objects. It is supportive of the right of every living being to fulfil its goal and to realise its destiny. Believer of Ahimsa knows the pain of others— *"Vaishnav Jan To Tene Kahiye Je Peed Paraayi Jaane Re"*. Ahimsa acknowledges the sacredness and inviolability of every life. For many, practice of nonviolence frees oneself from blemishes of karma and liberates one from the cycle of reincarnation. The doctrine of Ahimsa believes that Righteousness is the sustaining force of the Universe and Truth would ultimately triumph. For Gandhiji, Ahimsa was another form of truth.

Mahatma Gandhi put in practice this doctrine in public life and it manifested in Satyagraha. He found it an adequate enough weapon to face a mighty State. It rekindled millions of hearts; people from every walk of life joined the movement; a Nation of many religions and many languages bonded together to achieve the common goal of Independence. Gandhiji was the unifying force; his Satyagraha led to women empowerment; self-reliance and basic education. His frail physical frame betrayed strength of the lion and countrymen conquered fear.

Some thoughts of the Mahatma have been incorporated in our Constitution in the Directive Principles of State Policy. These include Directions for promoting welfare of the people by securing a social order through justice—social, economic and political—and to minimise inequalities in income, status, facilities and opportunities; promoting cottage industries; educational and economic interests of protect SCs, STs, and other weaker sections of the society from social injustice and exploitation; prohibiting consumption of intoxicating drinks and drugs; ensuring participation of workers in the management of industries. All these Directions aim at creation of a polity free from violence and injustice.

However, we need to have a look at how the State's been performing to promote nonviolence. Unfortunately, a mighty State very often is pitted against a weak individual - struggling, running from pillar to post to get what he is entitled to. The states has been a compulsive litigant against its own citizens. This obsession - far from Ahimsa - doesn't seem to wane. The state is steadily getting intolerant to legitimate criticism.

Instances of attacks on RTI activists unearthing corruption keep happening. Cases of rape and murder are rising. Odisha reported 2984 cases of rape and 1470 cases of murder in 2020 against 2950 and 1356 cases respectively the year before. Liquor and drugs seem to be flooding the state and crimes keep shooting up, particularly against women and children.

State's political leaders cutting across party lines remembered Mahatma Gandhi's first visit to the state a hundred years ago, on the 23rd of March, 1921. The state Assembly paid rich tributes to the Mahatma and passed a Resolution pressing for inclusion of Ahimsa in the

Preamble to the Indian Constitution stating that it would be the greatest tribute to the Father of the Nation.

But governance in Odisha has to do a lot to come meaningfully close to nonviolence and compassion. Powerful forces of avarice, intolerance, vengeance continue to be on the prowl. It is sheer tokenism to limit our homage to the Mahatma to a resolution to enshrine "Nonviolence" in the Constitution. Ahimsa has a chance to win only if it is practised as a way of life.

❏

River Mahanadi – Victim of Apathy for two Decades

While India's public dialogue veers mostly around politics, emotions and obscurantism, worthy topics like governance, economics or development crave for space despite the Prime Minister striving to bring issues like startups, Swachha Bharat, Make in India and Digital India to the centre-stage. Political strategists sometimes work overtime to create new issues, whip up emotions and resort to dramatics.

While Odisha continues to reel under poverty, unemployment, a chaotic health delivery system and a highly fragile education infrastructure despite bountiful natural endowments and a popular Chief Minister getting massive popular mandates, Chhattisgarh, a fledgling member in the comity of states in the Indian federal system, however, is proving the protagonists of smaller states right. Governance, on a mission mode, is geared towards development and prosperity despite the state having its various problems including a share of Maoist activism. Raipur has emerged as one of India's major manufacturing hubs.

Despite suffering an underperforming government, Odisha society continues to be peaceful and its people have learnt to make adjustments for survival --- like Dhana Majhi silently walking miles, carrying his dead wife on his shoulder or thousands of Odias regularly leaving homes for jobs of any type in distant places like Surat, Cochin or Bengaluru. Then suddenly political managers get active and a charade is raised about Chhattisgarh taking away their share of Mahanadi water. Women take out processions with water pitchers to pour water into the Mahanadi. Political workers stop Chhattisgarh bound trains, to make a point, putting unwarranted strain on India's federal fabric. An avoidable refrain on jingoism is created. Other political forces in the state look askance and plead for a united stand to protect the state's interest in case injustice has been done. The Party in power, however, opts to make the programme a Party affair and keeps other political Parties out.

How exactly has Odisha, the state downstream, been wronged is difficult to understand. The two states seem to have different perceptions on the use of the mighty River that discharges over twenty lakh cusecs of fresh water into the Bay of Bengal during monsoon—a volume, at par with the monsoon discharge of the Ganga. While Chhattisgarh has embarked upon judicious use of the abundant resource of the River-- that originates from the state— Odisha, in twenty two years of the BJD Government, has let the water either to flow into the sea or flood the delta—the largest in the Indian peninsula .

The 858 kilometre long River traverses 286 kilometres in Chhatisgarh and then flows in Odisha for 572 kilometres before joining the Sea at Paradip. Out of its total catchment of 141,600 square kilometres, 52.9 % is in Chhattisgarh and 46.3%, in Odisha. Up to Hirakud Dam, the River has a catchment of 83,400 sq kms of which 89.9% is in Chhattisgarh and 8.8%, in Odisha. Mahanadi's annual flow account for 59.16 Billion Cubic Metre (BCM), of which 29.90 BCM is from catchment in Odisha-- about 49% of the total water availability.

The river holds unlimited possibility for Odisha's prosperity. After ten lakh Odias died of starvation one hundred fifty six years ago in the Odisha Famine of 1866, canal irrigation was introduced using the water resource of the River. Thereafter, the massive Hirakud Dam was commissioned in 1957. Second phase of Delta Irrigation expanding the irrigation network came three decades later.

A comprehensive project to tap the full hydroelectricity potential of the river (2000MW), to ensure optimum use of the River's irrigation potential and also to ensure complete flood control, was drawn up and the foundation stone for the Tikarpara Dam was laid by the Prime Minister, Pandit Nehru. It, however, had to be abandoned as people opposed it. The project would have led to submersion of three towns and 1200 villages. The extent of submersion could have been reduced by lowering the height of the dam. This, however, would have reduced the hydro power generating capacity of 2000 MW substantially. Twenty years later, in 1985, attempt was made to build a Dam, at Manibhadra, downstream Tikarpara. This too had to be abandoned due to people's opposition to submersion of two towns and 273 villages.

A satisfactory engineering solution to the flood-problem in the delta had not been found till 1999. Could there be a design that would not lead to submergence of any town, not lead to submergence of any village permanently and would not lead to submergence of forests? Fortunately for us, such a blueprint has been prepared by a team of dedicated engineers led by an Engineer of outstanding merit and vision, Shri Pravat Kumar Misra, a former Engineer-in Chief of Government of Orissa. The plan envisages a

724 meter long barrage from Puta Hill to Ranitala Hill; a 2400 meter long dam --20 meter high (average height)-- from Manibhadra hill to Subalaya hill and 2200 meter long dykes joining Subalaya hill with Puta hill and Ranital hill with Mitcalfpur hill; right head regulator to provide irrigation to the right side of the Subalaya barrage and protective embankment rings around 73 villages with road connections to higher levels (cost- Rs 640 crore). At a later phase there would be provision for power generation of 210 MW during monsoon but power generation of 14 MW during non-monsoon period by making use of the release of power house release from the Hirakud dam (cost- Rs.630 crore). In the intermediate phase, the project would get the irrigation component to ensure irrigation to 140,000 hectares with provision for contributing about 1400 cusecs to the Rushikulya basin (cost- Rs450 crore). All the three phases would cost about Rs 1720 crore only. This estimate may have to be revised now; but the figures have been mentioned to highlight the economic way by which the entire flood problem could be tackled permanently.

The proposed Subalaya barrage is designed to reduce the maximum flood peak of 17.4 lakh cusecs on the basis of 100 years probability to only 8.7 lakh cusecs at the head of the Mahanadi delta. This would be possible through dynamic storage from the conservation level of 54.9 meter to the maximum level of 77 meters and back again to the conservation level within a period of six days and six hours (in case of a 100 year probability based maximum flood). In this situation, 73 villages would remain below the flood level for a maximum period of a little over six days Cuttack city remains below the high flood level for considerably longer periods almost every year behind the protective earthen embankments.

The existing infrastructure for flood moderation of the Mahanadi is the Hirakud Reservoir which has a modest live storage capacity of 3.9 million acre feet against the flood volume of 20 million acre feet of a typical flood in the Mahanadi. Therefore the huge population in the delta of the river continues to be vulnerable to the ravages of flood even after seven decades of the creation of the Hirakud reservoir.

Let us appreciate the gravity of the flood in the delta by looking at one part of the Mahanadi delta. This part is influenced by the Kuakhai River. This river divides into three rivers, namely, Bhargavi, Daya and Kushabhadra. These three rivers influence a very large area. The maximum combined carrying capacity of the three rivers is one lakh cusecs. When there is a normal flood peak of 9.60 lakh cusecs in the undivided Mahanadi at the head of the delta, the Kuakhai, as per given geometry, takes a share of 1.30 lakh cusecs which is 30 % in excess of the carrying capacity. This additional quantity spills through escape structures provided for the purpose. As a result, flood water flows into unprotected area resulting in water logging, crop damage and rendering large area unfit for cultivation. Inflow of the Mahanadi at the head of the delta at 8.70 lakh cusecs is considered as no distress flood as the river embankments downstream can carry this volume of water. In 1982, we, however, had a huge flood when the inflow at the head of the Delta was 15.87 lakh cusecs. This would indicate the magnitude of flood the delta has remained vulnerable to despite the Dam at Hirakud and yet a satisfactory solution has not been made.

With Subalaya barrage in place, there would be a completely different situation. The three branches of the Kuakhai would get a maximum flood peak of less than one lakh cusecs. Lateral spill of flood water would be a thing of the past. Further, passage of flood within the natural river channels for long periods of time would improve the hydraulic efficiency of the channels which would be helpful in removing the river mouth congestion.

Mahanadi delta is the largest river delta in peninsular India and is home to about a third of the state's population. Every year crores of rupees are spent on flood protection. After every major flood, government spends a big sum of money on relief and rehabilitation. Should such ad hoc response be accepted as the most humane way of tackling the flood issue in the Mahanadi delta or the government should perform its obligatory responsibility of distress removal? It is ironic that the state government keeps demanding from the centre a huge amount of money for relief and rehabilitation when the state reels under the fury of flood but would not take up the Subalaya project which would bring permanent remedy.

The other issue is regarding the management of this inter-state River. Have the ongoing River related projects in Chhattisgarh been injurious to Odisha's interest? The issue needs to be viewed in its entirety. One could argue that an upstream state could block the lean season river flows and alter the river flow regime drastically converting the River to a dry one, except during floods. It is, however, nobody's case that during monsoon months the River would not have enough water for Hirakud reservoir. In fact the reservoir, in its present capacity, can hold only about 16% of the flow. What is critical is the non-monsoon flow on which various activities in Odisha depend, including power generation, irrigation -- even hundreds of kilometres downstream, in the Delta, drinking water, and use by industries.

The High level Technical Committee under the

chairmanship of the former CWC Chairman, Shri R. Jeyaseelan to study various aspects of water usage for Hirakud Reservoir appointed in 2007 by Odisha Government, had, inter alia, observed that the non-monsoon average annual inflow to the Reservoir between 1951 and 1981 has been 2.750 million acre feet (MAF) whereas the same for the period between 1982 and 2006 has been 3.601 MAF. (Increase of 23.65%). Unless Odisha Government has any data to show that after 2006, the non-monsoon flow into the Hirakud Reservoir has substantially come down; the available data would only indicate that there is no need for panic.

Let us desist from using our Rivers for politics. Let us not invent "Disputes". Widely articulated assertions that Dams and Barrages in Chhattisgarh would make the river downstream go dry or affect flora and fauna in Chilka lake or the Bhitarakanika and Gahiramatha sanctuaries only betray insufficient knowledge on the River.

Now the River is the subject of dispute and the Tribunal is seized of the matter. It is difficult to know when the Award would be available. Even now it would be still worthwhile for both the states agree to meet and discuss the entire issue with open mind. One can hope that peace and development would emerge winner. Both the states have immense potential. People of both the states have hundreds of years of close bonding. There is enough water to meet the requirement of both the states. A joint Consultative mechanism under the existing legal framework surely can be put in place to address genuine concerns of both the states. Let the row not provide justification for continued inaction over the river related irrigation and flood control projects in Odisha. It is better Odisha left the River row behind and moved ahead. ❑

Bureaucracy is about Being Humane, Humble and Sensitive

Certain beliefs give both life and living a new dimension. I am not discussing on beliefs that could have religion connect. The beliefs I am talking about are secular, a part of art of living. As a child, a bruise while playing with friends pained less when friends sat around you and said comforting words. Empathy helps. It spreads a feel-good ambience and the small world around us looks cheerful. Having good wishes for not only your near and dear ones but for strangers, for living creatures around, and even inanimate objects one grows up with, like a hillock in front of your home, a building you pass by, a sapling being planted, add a positive dimension to life and living. You cherish health and prosperity all around. Your thoughts for a mango tree you pass by every morning while walking is for its wellbeing and bearing fruits in abundance, for being a perfect home to the cuckoos to sing and make the world around you cheerful and musical.

We are not born to live a life of isolation, withdrawal, keeping to ourselves and suspicious of others. We are not destined to be creatures of darkness. We are born to be in light, to radiate positive energy, to activate and refine our latent ability to flourish and benefit others. Such a mindset propels us to be on a continuous learning mode. There is no room for comparing us with others. Living is an open-ended journey toward excellence. Learning the power of gratitude is an extremely enriching experience. It makes us humble; it improves our ability for healing that transcends our suffering and moves us towards wholeness.

These qualities are embellishments that make us more humane, more productive and add purpose to our life. These are equally essential for public servants as well. With these qualities, they become more effective and highly motivated. They are more successful because they see the core purpose of the job at hand. The following example illustrates the pitfall of a mechanical attitude of a civil servant. It's about a building housing a grassroots level public office.

The office building of the Bhubaneswar urban ICDS project located in the area I live, finally got a functional compound wall with a good-looking gate, some days ago. Why it made an event for me one would ask. Here is why it did.

I had worked as Director, Community Development and Panchayati Raj years ago, in the Seventies, when Integrated Child Development Services (ICDS) Programme was in infancy with only a few block-level projects on ground and a few in the pipeline. Urban ICDS project came later. ICDS was a flagship programme of state intervention in the area of children and expectant and lactating mothers, their nutritional requirements and education of pre-school children. I had liked the programme immensely and that fondness survived decades of being away from it.

The Bhubaneswar office building may have come up at least some decades ago. It stood forlorn, without a compound wall. The office does have a storage godown where feeding materials are stocked. The public office is mostly visited by ladies connected with the programme. The office was on my morning walk route and every morning I was sensitive to its vulnerability and helpless existence. Things took a turn for the better when government buildings came up on three sides of this building. Walls on three sides were built by departments that owned the buildings. This was some years ago. Finally, the gap in front was built, perhaps, a month ago and a good gate adorned it a fortnight later.

This development for me was no less important than the completion of an important city flyover. Why the crucial infrastructure was missing for decades points to the need for greater sensitivity in our bureaucracy.

❏

Cotton Farming in Odisha

India, world's largest cotton producer, grows cotton in 122 lakh ha (8.74% of the country's net sown area) and produces now over 361 lakh bales of 170 kgs. While the yield rate varies from state to state, Gujarat's average yield is high- over 700 kg/hectare. Maximum production is from Gujarat, Maharashtra and Telangana. The crop is grown in Rajasthan, Haryana, Karnataka, Andhra, Madhya Pradesh, Punjab, Tamilnadu and Odisha as well.

Cotton in Odisha can be viewed as a significant force that has edged out less remunerative crops like Suan, Gulji, Arhar, Ragi and local upland Paddy grown on highlands in the western and southern parts of the state- a noteworthy silent though slow revolution, brought about not by government initiative but by proactive companies in the business of seeds and enterprising farmers from a neighbouring state. A major non-traditional commercial crop, it is presently grown in 1.69 lakh ha, that is, 2.73% of the state's total cropped area and 5.8 % of the state's total highland under crop. Present production is 4.65 lakh bales of 170 kg each −1.38% of the country's production – and productivity is 495 kg/ha (98.80% of the country's productivity). Most cotton is grown in Kalahandi, Bolangir, Rayagada and Nuapada though it is grown to some extent in Ganjam, Sonepur, Gajapati, Boudh, Bargarh, Phulbani and

Koraput as well. Most cotton growers are small, marginal farmers and lack resources to improve farming quality. The crop is wholly rain fed.

While these developments had been happening, Government should have been more than a disinterested onlooker. Bt cotton, which is resistant to bollworms, is yet to be officially allowed for cultivation in Odisha. A large number of hybrids are cultivated lacking fibre quality information. Absence of an appropriate policy for cultivation of Bt cotton in the state has been a constraint on legal action against delinquent seed sellers. Regional Research and Technology Transfer Station (RRTTS) of OUAT at Bhawanipatna, the only research centre for cotton in Odisha, in operation since 2001, came out with a new variety BS 279 that has been released in 2019 for cultivation. For a high-density planting system, variety BS 30,has also been released. There is a need for speedy action by the government for seed production to ensure wide availability of these new seeds.

Drip irrigation would help farmers and the crop. A tailor-made policy with adequate subsidy to small and marginal farmers should be put in place soon. It's high time for a holistic view of the Textile sector in the state. Spinning Mills set up years ago are now in shambles. Existing Ginning Mills are not adequate enough. There is a need for oil extraction facility as well.

Districts like Sundargarh, Mayurbhanj and Keonjhar provide ideal soil and climatic conditions for cotton. Cultivation should spread to these areas. Intercropping of pulses like red gram, black gram and oilseeds like soybean in cotton will increase the area of these pulses, improve soil health and reduce the risk for the cotton crop.

A well thought out road map is the need of the hour. That should comprise policy towards Bt Cotton; seed multiplication of new varieties released by OUAT, expansion of cotton cultivation to six lakh hectares; drip irrigation facility; ginning mills, spinning mills and oil extraction facilities.

Cotton holds out decent livelihood opportunity for six lakh small and marginal farmers of the state who presently struggle with less remunerative crops in uplands – an opportunity we can ill afford to miss.

❑

Odisha's Ecotourism

Odisha's overall performance in getting tourists, both domestic and international, has been modest. Of the 185.50 crore domestic tourists in the country in 2018, Odisha attracted only 1.52 crore – a measly 0.82%; and out of 2.89 crore international tourist arrivals, Odisha had a share of 0.38% with only 1.11 lakh visitors. That year, Jharkhand hosted 3.54 crore domestic tourists and 1.76 lakh foreign tourists and Tamilnadu, the most preferred destination-- both for domestic and foreign tourists-- had 38.59 crore domestic and 60.64 lakh foreign tourists. Odisha continues to be of marginal interest for tourists, both domestic and foreign

This realisation warranted a relook at the sector. Government now seems eager to go off the beaten track and is looking at ecotourism as a route to give the state a different image and offer access to more visitors to hidden treasures of the state. The way it has chosen to achieve the objective, however, raises concern. This needs a little explaining.

Through ecotourism, we create awareness and empathy for culture and environment and facilitate their nourishment. Ecotourism encourages low impact visits to eco-sensitive areas and visitors love to use their spare time to work as volunteers towards the growth of the area. Such tourists could stay with local families to learn about social customs, festivities, style of living, eating and cooking habits. A healthy partnership develops, enriching the host and the guest. The host community has a new source of income. Many would find the source more remunerative and fulfilling than the traditional practice of earning small income through extraction of depleting natural resources.

The state government's initiative towards ecotourism however continues to be government-centric and bureaucrat-driven. This obsession hardly takes into account the failure of the government in managing tourist infrastructure so far. Government has developed 47 ecotourism destinations with 333 cottages for 705 persons. Number of visitors to these destinations has been rising. Government is looking for new sites including water bodies for boosting ecotourism. A few trekking routes are also being developed. New destinations are to be managed by the local community including Self Help Groups and Vana Sanrakshana Samitis. These initiatives, however, do not address the core philosophy of ecotourism as discussed above. Standards prescribed by the International Ecotourism Society and the International Union for Conservation of Nature stipulate that visitors to natural environment would do nothing to change or adversely affect these areas; they should offer cultural and economic advantages to local communities.

Odisha, however, expanded the experiment of the previous year with the Eco Retreat model in December 2020 and set up Camps in Konark, Bhitarkanika, Hirakud, Satkosia and Daringbadi. While the first one was a repeat location, the rest were off the beaten track. The Camp was in operation for 90 days in Konark and for 82 days in the other locations. Konark attracted 5512 guests; Satkosia 2088; Daringbadi 1924; Hirakud 1810 and Bhitarkanika 1414.

This initiative was on Viability Gap Funding arrangement. It's not clear if predetermined norms on standards and expenditure were set for private operators. Minister did not disclose in the legislature the names of the operators. At the end of the show, the Government paid Rs 24 crore to bridge the viability gap. Lion's share was for Konark where the gap was a huge Rs 13.22 crore. This means a Guest (a fabulously rich person) in Konark was subsidised to the extent of Rs 24,000/-!!

A historic incident that underlined the attitude to wasteful public expenditure is worth recalling. In 1979, the launching of SLV programme had failed and the satellite fell into the sea soon after the launch. Shri Abdul Kalam was in charge of the project. He was overtaken by gloom because close to Rs 20 crore of public money got wasted. In contrast, the profligacy amounting to Rs 24 crore was a non-issue for the government and the Minister announced government's decision to repeat the model in future!! It is doubtful if any public good was achieved by this reckless experiment which was in complete deviation of the standards set by the International Ecotourism Society and the International Union for Conservation of Nature.

Considering the huge tourist traffic of the country, development of a few eco camps to attract tourists is just baby step and it is most unlikely to make a difference to the tourist arrivals in Odisha. What Odisha seems to be predominantly doing in the garb of ecotourism is pampering consumerism in the cradle of nature, compromising its splendour and serenity instead of using the ecotourism model to nurture and develop scenic spots through guest-host partnership and low impact footfalls.

❑

Farm Ecosystem of Odisha Remains Weak

In 1992, that is about 30 years ago, as Agriculture Secretary of Odisha Government, I had visited Nasik, Dhule and Jalgaon region of Maharashtra and looked at the agricultural development. This region gets an annual rainfall of only 18 inches. In May, the temperature goes beyond 45 degree Celsius. Adverse climatic conditions have not discouraged the spirit of enterprise in the farmers. Through adoption of drip irrigation and taking recourse to scientific management, they had been getting a per hectare yield of 715 quintals of banana, 100 quintals of grapes, 250 quintals of pomegranates, 200 quintals of mango, 300 quintals of orange and 150 quintals of lemon. My interaction with a few entrepreneurs afforded insight into their indomitable spirit, application of science and technology and the thrill of excellence that took them and their society quite far on the road to prosperity.

On 27th of June, I reached Nasik and visited the tomato fields of the farmer, Shri K.K.Patil. He had grown tomato in five acres out of which three acres had been covered through drip irrigation. Shri Patil was expecting 30 tons of tomato per acre from the irrigated land. After harvesting tomatoes, he would grow Chilli and thereafter, again grow Tomato. I visited the farm of Shri Firoze Masani in Nasik, a Chartered

Accountant by profession who worked in Europe, but for personal reasons, came back to Nasik and took up floriculture. His poly-houses over an area of two and half acres under blooming Carnation through drip irrigation was a feast to the eyes. He had planted two lakh plants – all the seedlings had been imported from Holland. On an average, he harvested eighteen flowers from a plant. Most of his flowers got exported to Holland while the markets in Mumbai, Ahmedabad and Pune absorbed some. Another entrepreneur, Sri Bogul, had grown strawberry in seven acres of land. He had planted thirty thousand strawberry seedlings per acre and covered the entire plantation under drip irrigation. He had timed the operation in such a manner that the strawberry from his farm would be available in European markets in December when strawberry from no other country reached the market. Shri Harish Chandra Jagtap was one of the hundreds of enterprising grape growers of Nasik. He had grown grapes in forty four acres of land. On an average, he harvested twelve tons of grapes per hectare. Along with some other grape growers of the area, they had started a Cooperative Society which set up a Champagne factory and champagne was being exported. They had been regularly exporting grapes to Europe. Pre-cooling chambers had been set up at different places close to grapevines so that freshly harvested grapes got into the pre-cooling chambers without loss of time. Subsequently, the grapes got transferred to containers for export to foreign markets.

Wakode village, at a distance of ten kilometers from Ajanta, was where I met a young agriculture scientist, Sri Nitin Phadke, engaged in growing Teak through drip irrigation. This seemed to me a novel experiment. He had planted 5,400 saplings per acre and the plants, growing very close to one another, were struggling to get adequate sunlight and therefore growing fast. Assuming mortality of 25%, he would be able to grow 4,050 plants per acre. Through drip irrigation he was also providing chemical fertilizer to the plants. Shri Phadke was cutting off unnecessary branches and, thereby inducing the plants to grow taller. After four years, the scientist would harvest 1350 trees and earn Rs.67,500 /- @ Rs.50/- per plant. Thereafter he would wait for four years and harvest 1350 eight-year-old trees and earn Rs.2,70,000/- @ Rs.200/- per tree. After four years he would harvest 675 trees and earn Rs.6, 75,000/- @ Rs.1000/- per tree. After four years, he would sell the balance 675 trees at Rs.6, 000/- per tree and would have a gross income of Rs.36, 50,000/-. His total income in sixteen years would be Rs.46,62,500/-.

Even today, we in Odisha have not reached this level of performance they had achieved three decades ago. We love to set our own pace, oblivious of what is going on around. We love blowing out trumpet; giving big shout out to baby steps. In five years of operation of the 'Per Drop More Crop' component of the Centrally sponsored PMKSY- PDMC Scheme, while Karnataka brought 9.25 lakh ha under Drip Irrigation, Andhra 7.43 lakh ha and Maharashtra 5.41 lakh ha; Odisha achieved a measly coverage of 29.143 ha.

Some states create more wealth through Agriculture than through Industry. Contribution of Agriculture to State GDP is higher than of Industry in states like West Bengal, Maharashtra, Madhya Pradesh and Andhra Pradesh. The disparity in production and productivity keeps growing, pushing Odisha to suboptimal stage of return from farming. In 2013-14, while Odisha produced Banana worth Rs 241 crore; Tamilnadu's was worth Rs 5970 crore and Rs 3720 crore for Maharashtra. Though share of Agriculture in Odisha GDP has gone up to 27%, it would be relevant to quantify it and compare it with Maharashtra. Odisha's SGDP of Rs 5.34 lakh crore got a share of Rs 1.44 lakh crore from Agriculture compared to Maharashtra Agriculture contributing Rs 6.99 lakh crore (25%) to its SGDP of Rs 27.96 lakh crore (India's richest state). In other words, farming sector of Maharashtra contributed five times more than what Odisha did.

Given the quality of soil, availability of water and burgeoning demand, it is absolutely possible to scale up production and productivity and enrich the farming community. Political leadership, however, is yet to grasp the potential the sector holds and the way it can contribute to equitable wealth creation. I am yet to hear the Chief Minister expressing publicly his desire to see the huge Rice fallows on either side of the Railway Line or National Highway between Berhampur and Jaleswar, under intense agricultural activity throughout the year. The wasteland experience ends the moment one enters Andhra or West Bengal. Odisha must stop romanticising poverty. Odisha's ailing Farm Eco-system needs appropriate retrofit to be vibrant. Our farmers can surely perform if political leadership motivated them and bureaucrats did meaningful handholding.

❑

Mo Cycle Project in Bhubaneswar

Despite exponential use of automobiles for public and private transport, around 30% of daily trips in India are said to be made either on foot or by cycle. This segment needs to be nurtured and protected with better facilities on roads. Cycle continues to be the preferred conveyance of the poor; but the number of cycle riders belonging to well-to-do segments of society is on the rise as well. These people take to cycling for leisure, endurance exercise and for their concern for environment. India's huge young population should be oriented towards cycle as the ideal transport mode for short trips as well as a pastime on holidays. Compared to other public transportation projects, cycle sharing systems, fortunately, remain inexpensive. Cycle sharing systems can conveniently be dovetailed into conventional public transport arrangements for providing first and last-mile connectivity. The National Urban Transport Policy, keeping in mind the need for public bicycle sharing system, speaks about "movement of people and not vehicles". Ministry of Urban Development has come up with a toolkit to promote cycle share systems in India. India's thriving bicycle industry could be an important stakeholder in the emerging city cycling revolution.

A pilot project in Mumbai, 'Cycle Chalao', started in 2011 with 30 cycles, was operational on 2.5 km between Mulund East Railway Station and Vaze Kelkar College.

This was an instant hit among young commuters. It helped commuters who got out of buses and trains and then had to settle for a costly auto-rickshaw and taxi ride to reach home or place of work located within one to two km.

Soon thereafter, Pune Municipal Corporation through 'Cycle Chalao' ran and operated a public cycle share system in the city. However, the project ran into rough weather. Cycle Chalao wound up their initiative and was of the view that Bicycle sharing systems to be successful in India have to be fully sponsored by the public authorities and private associates should act as contractors to provide construction, operations and maintenance. On August 6, 2012, Namma Cycle, a cycle share system was launched at the Indian Institute of Science, Bengaluru.

Subsequently, more cities like Bhubaneswar, Mysore, Jaipur, Rajkot, Vadodara and Ahmedabad, were found expressing interest in Bicycle sharing arrangement. Bhubaneswar even sent officials to Amsterdam to see the facilities provided to cyclists.

On November 26, 2018, Chief Minister flagged off a promotional rally of 300 Bicycle enthusiasts from Bhubaneswar Airport Square to Kalinga Stadium and Odisha experienced yet another innovative community facility as a part of the transformational Smart City initiative. The city had its Public Bicycle Sharing (PBS) Project, christened as Mo Cycle. It arrived in the city that was hosting the Hockey World Cup Tournament, two days later.

Bhubaneswar Smart City Limited (BSCL) brought 1000 Hexi Bikes, 500 Yaana and 500 Yulu Bikes. Little was done towards creating adequate infrastructure for the 2000 sophisticated Bicycles. It was out and out impulsive financial adventurism; procuring 2000 expensive Cycles in one go. Panchkula was a success story with just 200 Cycles and Bhopal, a much larger city, had settled for 500 cycles.

Mo Cycle system was to reduce traffic congestion, enhance road-space efficiency, and improve air quality in the city. The intent was also to increase accessibility of PBS by providing first and last-mile connectivity. Planners opted for a dense network of stations instead of keeping the bike stations only at major destinations or junctions. Through this innovation, they wanted to connect the 'Sources' to 'Destinations' and therefore bike stations were set up within residential areas as well as on main streets so that people could start and get back to their homes on a bicycle. With many bicycles coming in they were confident of building a robust PBS and bicycle culture.

Little did they think about the prevailing chaos on roads of Bhubaneswar where, as on March 31, 2021, there were 10.71 lakh two-wheelers and 2.59 lakh four-wheelers, leaving little space for cycles to move. Precious little was done to lay dedicated cycle tracks; no serious move was made to make marked cycling space on roads free from truant bikers. The induction of 2000 bicycles into the turbid space was like writing an essay on pandemonium.

Naturally, soon after the launch, number of users kept falling rapidly—from 37,008 in December 2018 to 6216 in March 2019. It soon became clear that the government that launched the programme was only keen on inauguration and advertisement rather than creating credible infrastructure in the city for cycles to move.

Hundreds of Mo Cycles were found rotting at docking stations across the city; unseemly squabbles between the Smart City Authority and the Suppliers became louder.

Maintenance of the GPS enabled Cycles suffered; the public felt let down. Yet another government scheme was getting dysfunctional soon after a well-hyped inauguration show, signalling 'a City on Move'. Smart City Authority transferred the scheme to the Municipal Corporation in October 2020, within two years of launch. Number of cycles in operational condition kept plummeting, so did the number of users.

Meanwhile, the State unit of BJP alleged poor management of the cycle service and irregularity in procurement of Mo Cycles. BJP legal cell coordinator even talked of taking the matter to Court seeking a transparent investigation.

At present, the PBS seems to be totally dysfunctional. Some attempts, however, are being made towards maintenance and improve the stock of functional cycles. It would be unfortunate if the Bhubaneswar PBS is written off. Stakeholders should work towards reviving it.

A well-designed cycle sharing scheme is socially useful; but there are challenges. Apart from political will, the scheme needs dedicated allocation of government funds for cycling infrastructure. More users from well-to-do segments of society making use of PBS would address the issue of cycling being poor man's choice. Bhubaneswar has now a huge number of morning walkers and joggers. Their number seems to be rising fast. City gyms too remain reasonably patronised. Cycling, as a morning exercise, could be appealing if it is well planned. A ride from Mukteswar Temple to Chaushathi Yogini Temple at Hirapur across the Kuakhai by keeping one lane of the Two-lane Road reserved for cyclists between five and eight in the morning could bring in a new cycling culture in the city. There could be other stretches in the city for the same objective as well.

However, cycle sharing system to emerge as a means to provide first and last-mile connectivity in Bhubaneswar would depend on when the city can have safe and dedicated cycle tracks. In the meantime, we may focus on certain educational campuses like IIT, a few Engineering and Medical Colleges for students and teachers using the PBS.

Bhubaneswar Roads have almost been chocked by motor-bikes. Stringent registrations of new motor-bikes perhaps would help. It should be possible to work out a viable PBS for Bhubaneswar through better maintenance of cycles, reducing the number of cycle stations and reducing the number of cycles by half. Since Rourkela is another Smart city, it could as well take a few Mo Cycles from Bhubaneswar and introduce cycling culture in the Steel City.

❑

Hyder Encounter – Gory End to a Violent Life

Sheikh Hyder, the widely known gangster, met with a gory death in the afternoon of July 24,2021 on his way to Baripada Jail from the Jail at Choudwar. The shifting reportedly was as per orders of the Court. Hyder who was serving a life sentence fell to bullets fired by one of the ten policemen escorting him to Baripada. The incident was widely reported in the media as an encounter.

The incident does raise the important issue of Right to Life. The Constitution of India does not make any difference between the life of a Saint and a Villain. I am not on the question of how virtuous or vicious the dead man was. Article 21 of the Constitution of India does not expressly say about custodial death, but its ambit is wide. This Fundamental Right states that no person shall be deprived of his life except according to the procedure established by law. The issue here is was the gunning down of Sheikh Hyder in accordance with the procedure established by law.

Reportedly, Hyder snatched away an AK-47 Rifle from one of the policemen and threatened to kill the policemen in case they resisted his escape. A Sub-Inspector of Police fired at him from his Revolver severely injuring him. Presumably, Hyder was escaping armed with the

AK-47 Rifle. In that case his posterior would have been hit; not anterior. Police will have to do a lot of explaining why he was hit on the chest. Hyder was serving life imprisonment and would have continued in confinement indefinitely. With his background of criminal activities over decades, society was safer with him in jail rather than in freedom. For various reasons he was shifted from one jail to another, a number of times. He has been travelling while undergoing jail-term for medical consultations and treatment as well. He perhaps had not attempted an escape earlier while he was travelling. However, he planned well to flee from custody some months ago when he was under treatment at the Medical College at Cuttack where he was accommodated in an air-conditioned room. Accomplices reportedly were many, ranging from compliant police personnel and relatives to lady acquaintances. Police had drawn flak over this issue and sprang into action swiftly.

He was nabbed near Hyderabad and brought back. The escape, however, did point to serious dereliction of duty by a number of government functionaries across Departments and an independent investigation would have revealed a lot of skeletons in the government cupboard. It would suit many if these details remained a secret.

Hyder operated through efficient networking; took advantage of the soft underbelly of the prevailing political-administrative system and benefited from the slow pace of the criminal justice delivery arrangement. That in large number of cases Hyder was acquitted because there was no witness to depose against him, only indicates the power he enjoyed in his area of operation. His words prevailed where witnesses thought it prudent to remain silent and enjoy his protection rather than put their life to risk by standing behind law enforcement agencies.

He was worldly-wise to know that escape from police custody does need meticulous planning, accomplices, getaway vehicle, secure hideout. These logistics support would not be forthcoming just wherever he chose to get down from a police vehicle to attend to call of nature. Even if he had captured a Rifle, it did not guarantee a successful escape. If he was to shoot and kill the escorting policemen, he, armed with one AK 47 Rifle, as alleged, could have fired from a distance; not necessarily drawing himself too close to the target. The incident did not take place at night when an escape was easier. It was before four in the afternoon with clear daylight.

The incident looks rather a rarest of rare case where a person armed with one AK-47 Rifle about to trigger a volley of fire would fall to Revolver shots. The death does raise many issues the Police need to answer.

❏

The Lady Who Redefined the Art of Stalking Influencial Men

Suddenly, a lady from Kalahandi District, Archana Nag, became the talk of Bhubaneswar. Her story was one of rags to riches. While her fast journey to the world of affluence and luxury could be a case of ease of doing business in Bhubaneswar, it also revealed the underbelly of the capital city of a poor state of 45 million people most of whom are fed with one rupee rice even after 22 years of rule by the regional party.

The lady became the cynosure of the media and sensational stories kept coming in about her activities that brought her both wealth and status within a short time. She was supposed to have friends in right number and at right place. Her powerful patrons reportedly ranged from film producer to bureaucrats, from political leaders to affluent contractors. Involvement of more than a score of political personalities including some legislators, mostly belonging to the ruling party, was talked about.

Role of police was discussed as also issues like why the lady was arrested in a hurry, why she was not taken immediately to police remand for interrogation, why the many victims of her manipulations were not showing up before the police to narrate their stories and unravel secrets that helped Archana increase her wealth and influence.

Archana model of entrepreneurship, however, raises a few issues to ponder over. Its immediate impact is on the tenacious, the industrious, the highly educated youths who keep struggling awaiting Dame Luck's smile. They today stand disillusioned. One feels convinced that in the present state of decay of societal values, it's the sleazeball that has the highest chance of entrepreneurial success. Her facile success points to wilting of righteousness and the viscous emerging winner. Her case shows how wealth creation process need not necessarily have to be a painstaking and arduous task. It shows there are shortcuts to prosperity. These unpalatable realities unfortunately promote negativity in the society. Belief in rule of law and fairness in government diminishes.

If Government is committed to reversing this widely held perception, it must come down heavily on 'Archanas', their patrons and accomplices irrespective of their parentage, social and political connections. Police needs to be given a free hand to act swift and effective. Agencies handling economic offence matters need to act fast. The prevailing perception, however, is different. People, by and large, feel that the political characters, if involved, would most likely be protected and the present uproar would be made to subside. This impression is indicative of the pervading state of negativism and disappointment in an unjust society where the guilty is not necessarily punished.

It is this vital issue the Government of the day must address as this is about the essence of governance. Archana case is important for this reason. It is worth recalling that on the occasion of the Party's 20th Foundation Day in December 2017, Chief Minister and BJD President, Naveen Patnaik, exhorted his party members to be simple and high thinking and serve people, who, he said, were the 'ultimate masters'. He advised them to dedicate their lives to 'Maa, Mati and Manisa' (Mother, Motherland, People) and asked them to respect people's sentiment and meet the promises made to them. The reported involvement of quite a few of the ruling party legislators in the sordid saga of sleaze, however, runs counter to the Achar Samhita (Code of Conduct) prescribed by the Party's Supremo.

A word about Raj Dharma seems relevant at this juncture. "How should a King behave?" Yudhistira had asked Bhisma. "Righteousness," Bhisma answered, is the watch word of a King. His senses should be perfectly under control. Poison kills but one man, so does a weapon. But, Bhisma said, wicked counsels destroy an entire kingdom with kings and subjects. A king can easily become great by doing just two things: refraining from harsh speech and disregarding those that are wicked.

The wicked must be disregarded. The role of the party leaders involved must be thoroughly and swiftly probed and marching orders served on them. This is what the society wants; it wants to be reassured that crime does not pay. Naveen Patnaik with his stature and long years as Chief Minister and the party president owes it to the people who love him. Righteousness is the key word, to quote Bhisma. Raj Dharma is all about it. While everyone involved in this affair must be brought under the long arms of law, the party men involved must be politically punished and swiftly.

❏

Small Babus with Deep Pockets

Two recent raids of Odisha Vigilance - one relating to an Assistant Engineer in the irrigation division in Ganjam district and the other, relating to a Gram Rojgar Sevak (GRS) working on the outskirts of Bhubaneswar – which led to detection of huge assets, raise important issues like quality of governance and government's attitude and response to corruption. In case of the former, the engineer concerned was the all-important functionary in the division office where he was stationed for 22 years since the day he joined government service as a junior engineer.

Kartikeswar Roul, the Junior Engineer, was never transferred and wielded tremendous power and clout in the office. Searches resulted in the highest seizure of cash during any raid by the State Vigilance. It is to be noted that on April 7, 2022, the second day of the house search, Rs 2.5 crore in cash was unearthed from his house and that of his second wife. Besides, assets worth over Rs 2.76 crore including two flats and one double-storey building in Bhubaneswar, bank and insurance deposits of about Rs 37.23 lakh, seven plots of land including two in the prime area of Bhubaneswar were unearthed. Roul has been arrested.

The case of the Gram Rojgar Sevak, Babuli Charan Padhihari is even more revealing. Babuli had joined the job not long ago and earned around Rs 6000 per month and this wage had increased to Rs 8500 when he was arrested by the Vigilance on charges of corruption. He came under Vigilance surveillance recently when he allegedly sold 18 plots of land in the suburbs of Bhubaneswar. His assets included costly buildings in the city suburbs, a car, a bike, and gold ornaments worth Rs 8 lakh. He was allegedly in possession of 59 plots of land in and around Bhubaneswar. He seemed to be liberally taking advantage of the Mahatma Gandhi National Rural Employment Guarantee Fund and was on an enrichment overdrive.

That a humble government employee not even on regular government pay scale could amass wealth of this proportion being posted so close to Bhubaneswar only betrayed a wholesome tolerant attitude to corruption and total delegation of important economic programme execution responsibility to petty officials, with the BDO and supervisory officials remaining occupied perhaps with more important responsibilities.

Case of Roul leads one to believe that the Government could let transferable officials remain in one station for decades if they were good at networking skill or were politically connected. The case of Padhihari revealed the steep slide of supervision responsibility of officials. Both cases raise the issue of the government's attitude to corruption of officials.

There are about 4 lakh government employees and it is likely that some would be deficient in probity and integrity. The supervising officers have a big role in ensuring efficiency and honesty in governance. The work of officials needs regular monitoring, and accountability needs to be ensured. There cannot be a kindly attitude, a forgiving disposition towards corruption. Corruption, in many cases, is an indicator of lack of supervision and in some cases indicates collusion of superiors.

As against about 4 lakh state government employees, the Vigilance set up in the state has limitations of both size and time. In 2020, Odisha Vigilance registered only 245 cases against 381 persons including 53 Class-I, 38 Class-II, 183 Class-III, five Class-IV officials, 26 public servants and 76 private individuals. Of these, 93 were disproportionate asset (DA) cases involving DA of Rs 124 crore in respect of 24 Class-I and 20 Class-II officers. Since 2019, Odisha government has compulsorily retired 158 government employees as of March 2022. However, investigation of many Vigilance cases takes a long time to complete; the rate of conviction is not high. Given these limitations, Vigilance has not been a strong enough deterrent. Much stronger vigil and administrative action seem called for. It is highly improbable that the corrupt practices of a subordinate official remain unknown to the superior officer. When the corrupt subordinate is caught, the superior hardly ever gets the blame whereas he too needs to be hauled up for dereliction of duty. If that was done, there would be better performance, less corruption and better utilization of government resources.

The issue of corruption in government had even engaged the attention of Kautilya. He had suggested a few measures which are worth considering even now. In cases of corruption, he had said, all concerned officials must be checked and the non-corrupt supporters should also be treated as corrupt. He had suggested regular transfer of public servants. He advocated strict application of law to prevent and control corruption.

It is worth recalling that the Biju Janata Dal had played the honesty card before coming to power in 2000. Liberal use of CBI was made to instill a sense of fear among the corrupt. The situation seems to be different now. Serious lapses and cases of graft of gargantuan proportion keep surfacing at seemingly innocuous quarters and lend support to the widespread belief that corruption has now engulfed the state like forest fire.

Corruption impacts delivery of services, it breeds societal anger and discontent. Steadily but surely, it transforms the huge governing apparatus to nonproductive asset (NPA). The government bears the cost of a corrupt employee by entertaining him in service but does not get his services the way it should have – a contingency any government should avoid. A much more effective strategy to curb corruption seems to be the need of the hour.

❏

Odisha's Modest MSME Sector

India's approximately 63 million MSMEs, that include about 2.5 million registered ones, contribute about 29% towards the GDP. The registered MSME units are dominated by 2.2 million micro enterprises with 0.24 million small enterprises and 10,981 medium enterprises. The sector presently provides employment to over 11 crore people. These productive units no doubt provide the backbone to our economy.

Khadi and Village Industries constitute a very important segment of this sector. While production of Khadi has more than doubled in five years and sales three times since 2015-16, Village Industry production has nearly doubled during this period. In 2019-20, turnover of Khadi and Village Industries was an impressive Rs 88,887 crore with Khadi fabric products sales reaching Rs 4211 crore.

The sector produces Khadi apparels and a wide range of products like pickles, honey, hand sanitisers, papad, oil, leather items, cosmetics, soaps and shampoos which are eagerly sought after by ever increasing number of discriminating consumers both within and outside the country. KVI Commission handles as many as 150 products with in-house capacity of excellence in fields like bee-keeping, pottery and bakery.

Country is now focused on a policy to bring a

transformative change in the villages through innovative, research-based technology, specially adapted for rural areas so as to increase MSME contribution to 40% of GDP and enable 15 crore people to work in this sector.

Over a period of about 75 years, migration of 30% of the country's population from rural areas has taken place due to lack of growth of the village economy. The present pandemic brought to sharper focus, the trials and tribulations the migrant workers faced. Creation of adequate job opportunities in India's villages would lead to revival of rural economy; arrest distress induced migration and would minimize loss of livelihood during calamities like the recent pandemic. Vocation like Bee keeping would not be hit by pandemic related shutdown whereas pavement selling would.

The MSME Ministry is actively working towards launching the e-commerce portal for MSMEs that will help them market and sell their products in India and internationally similar to platforms such as Amazon and Alibaba. The e-commerce portal called Bharat Craft was announced by the government around mid-2019. This would be a live gateway for MSMEs to take products to the global market.

Government already has a business-to-business e-Marketplace to help MSMEs sell to government organizations. With the launch of a government-owned B2C marketplace where MSMEs would be able to sell directly to consumers, Union Minister of MSME, Nitin Gadkari hopes, we "should soon see turnover on the platform to the tune of Rs 10 lakh crore in the next few years.

One of the major challenges faced by MSME owners is over delayed payments which lead to a working capital lockdown, which, in turn, creates a lot of mismanagement of resources, money, and operations. There is now concerted move to pay receivables within 45 days. Government of India is contemplating a law to address this issue.

Odisha's MSME sector has about 4.50 lakh entities with investment of about Rs 22000 crore and employs about 17 lakh people. Most units are micro enterprises. Sales turnover of the sector continues to be modest. The sector does provide livelihood to 17 lakh people but does not add much to their household wealth. Odisha Khadi & Village Industries Board continues to operate modest—with sales turnover of around Rs 2 crores in a year. Annually about 55,000 new MSMEs are coming up in the state which in itself reflects an urge to be entrepreneurial.

However, the state has a long way to go to have a reasonable share of the cake the sector offers. Potential of the state being huge, a road map for five years should be drawn that should plan for employment opportunities for about 60 lakh people and substantial scaling up of the sales turnover of Odisha Khadi and Village Industries Board to the level of at least Rs 1000 crore. These targets shouldn't be viewed as fancy targets as these takes into consideration the present level of activity the country has been able to achieve. We need to ponder why while India exported Natural Honey worth Rs 634 crore (59,537 MT), Odisha's total Honey sales in 2019-20 was worth only Rs 12 lakhs. Our performance must be transformative and sustainable to impact both livelihood and wealth creation.

❑

Governance Deficit Leads
to Migration from Odisha

As per informal estimates, over 2.5 million people from Odisha migrate to other states for livelihood. While industrialised states and mega cities have offered job opportunities to younger segments of unemployed persons of Odisha, thousands of people in acute economic distress have resorted to migration for jobs like brick making and moved to states like Andhra Pradesh, Tamil Nadu and Telangana.

Migration to work in brick kilns demonstrates human distress in most acute form. Children too are engaged in brick making while they ought to have been in school. These children when they grow up lose opportunities available to educated youths. Most workers do not get the wage and working environment promised during recruitment. Being away from home for over six months year after year bestow on these families a separate disadvantaged identity in their own villages and they lose out in integrating themselves with the economic and social development process taking place in their place of birth. Children are the worst victims in this process of disconnect.

Process of recruitment for brick kilns is pernicious, cruel, exploitative and clearly a system of bondage. The employer controls the employee by keeping him/her in debt and withholding wages. It is cunningly justified as being beneficial to the worker as, at the end of the season, it leaves with the worker a good amount of savings. The reality however, is the system allows the owner to control the supply of labour. If workers were paid at the end of each month their full wages, as required under law, most would be able to pay back at the end of the second month the large advances paid at the beginning.

National Human Rights Commission (NHRC) has been of the view that the concerned authority is duty bound to raise a presumption that labourers were bonded labourers if the employer had not maintained statutory records for workers. In case of migrant workers in brick kilns such a presumption would be absolutely legitimate. That such an unacceptable mode of distress migration keeps going demonstrates severe governance deficit. It cannot be justified on the ground that in the past too people of the region left homes with families to work in distant tea plantations. Times then were difficult; welfare government hadn't arrived. It would be therefore sheer insensitivity to view migration to brick kilns as a legacy issue.

Annual migration season commence regularly from parts of Bolangir, Nuapada, Kalahandi and Bargarh districts. Labour Sardars from different states arrive at centres like Kantabanji. They have an elaborate network and they lure vulnerable families in thousands. The situation has aggravated in last two decades, with no solution in sight. The zone of recruitment seems to be getting even larger and has spread even to the undivided Koraput District. This region of the state is marked by little industrial activity.

Government, unfortunately, seems to be viewing this unacceptable activity with a stoic attitude. To keep state intervention limited to a revamped MGNREGA by providing work for 300 days with a daily wage of Rs 308 would be highly inadequate. MGNREGA afflicted with usual nepotism and lack of commitment by executing agencies, has not been able to ensure adequate relief. Participation of household has been extremely disappointing. In the 20 critical blocks of Bargarh, Bolangir, Kalahandi and Nuapada, the programme had provided 100 days of work to less than 4000 households in 2018-19; less than 20,000 in 2019-20 and less than 80,000 in 2020-21. Less than 15,000 households could get 200 days of work and less than 200 had 300 days of work in 2020-21.

Distress induced migration to brick kilns is a story of cruel exploitation of the weak by the wily. The state has a role to play. A brief narrative on the role of state in such situations would be relevant. On February 23, 1994, Chief Minister, Biju Patnaik, was travelling to Rourkela on official work. I had accompanied him. The plane was overflying Bonai region of the state. "I had started my official career at Bonai in my first posting as the sub divisional officer (SDO)" I told the Chief Minister. "This is an area which is so rich in natural endowments and yet is economically so backward", I continued. He was listening with interest. Encouraged by his eagerness to listen, I thought of telling him what I thought should be an appropriate approach in governance in such areas." In our society, for those people who do not have strong power of discrimination, the state should act as a protector; people having power of discrimination well developed, should be free to shape their lives according to their volition and the state should act only as a facilitator. While formulating policy, government should keep this objective in view", I said. "As a young officer I had made many surprise visits to many liquor shops, both, licensed and unlicensed, selling country-liquor in Bonai sub-division at different times of day and night. Each visit had made me sad for I had noticed every liquor shops to be virtually a granary. A simple tribal would run short of money while consuming more liquor than what he could pay for and would, in a state drunkenness, pawn his crops to the liquor merchant. Most of the agricultural produce of a village would find its way to the liquor shop. In my view the state must protect the vulnerable section of the population. In the tribal areas government should abolish liquor shops. Of course, Government would thereby suffer some financial loss; but as Finance Secretary I assure you I would be able to absorb the loss. You alone can take a bold step in this regard" I told him with some emotion but with conviction. He listened but was quiet. The next day he made the historic announcement on the floor of the Assembly abolishing country liquor in the tribal area.

The state acting as protector for these poor families of Nuapada, Bolangir, Kalahandi and Bargarh who seem destined to work in brick kilns is yet to be demonstrated. To that extent government seems to be failing; but it must succeed.

New initiatives must have to be taken. A policy announcement by the Chief Minister that the state will not permit its people to migrate for working in brick kilns would surely help. The Sardars would surely stop coming to the state thereafter. Commercial Banks must be advised to come up with appropriate loan products to finance purchase of Smartphone, Computer, Television, Study Loan so that the need for an advance from the Sardar doesn't arise.

Farmers have been growing cotton, maize and oilseeds

for years but the region has remained bereft of downstream industries which could provide jobs in all seasons. A mission approach seems necessary to set up adequate number of maize processing units, ginning facilities and at least 20,000 power-looms in a cluster. Western Odisha Development Council has to spearhead these initiatives.

❑

Silk City Berhampur Awaits its Tryst with Destiny

The Italian entrepreneur, Signor Maglioni, who established the Hotel Palm Beach, in 1914 at Gopalpur, close to Berhampur, surely saw opportunity amidst the flourishing economic activity in the area. It was the first Beach Resort of the country and drew people from all around. Gopalpur was a thriving Port and was open to both foreign and coastal trade. Myrabolans were destined to London and Antwerp; Hemp to London while Rice, Oilseeds and Turmeric to Colombo. Arecanuts landed from Penang; Coconut oil from Galle, while Matches arrived from Christiania and Hamburg. Refined oil came from Colombo; Spirits & Wines from UK. There was sizeable traffic to/from Yangon (formerly known as Rangoon). The Port was of great use to the Army during both World Wars as the eastern post for strategy operations in respect of Yangon. Palm Beach Hotel naturally had brisk footfalls. Sea and River fisheries formed an important industry in Ganjam coast. Around the year 1900, there used to be 21 fish curing yards on the coast and their outturn was greater than any of the coastal Districts of India except two in the west coast. In 1903-04, nearly 3000 tons of fish were salted in these curing yards.

City of Berhampur had a population of 61,000 in 1950 when Vishakhapatnam city had just over a lakh of population. While the Andhra coastal city in 2021 is a thriving metropolis with a population of over 2.2 million, Berhampur, known for its exquisite silk Patta Sarees for centuries, has a population of just over four lakhs in 2021. The city, however, continues to be one of the most important commercial centres of the state, displaying varieties of micro level entrepreneurial skill of its industrious inhabitants through products ranging from Silk, Pickles, Papad to Brass and Horn works. It is the major Mango hub of the state and hosts many well patronised Restaurants serving ethnic food. The city is also home to a Government Medical College, and the renowned Khallikote College. Berhampur University is close by.

Berhampur is close to the Port, close to a few exquisitely serene Beaches; close to the Chilka Lake. Many important tourist spots too are nearby. These include Bhetnoi village, home to over 7000 Krushnasara Mruga (Black Buck) only 70 kilometers away; the scenic Taptapani (85 kms) in the cradle of the lush-green rolling hills of the Eastern Ghats; the picturesque Jirang (115 kms) township with its a thriving Tibetan population and Tara Tarini Temple (34 kms). The nearby Jaugada hosts the famous Rock Inscription of Emperor Ashoka.

The city's huge potential for growth, however, remains untapped. Compared to the thriving economic activities during good part of the 19th and early part of the 20th centuries that had ramifications even offshore through movement of people and merchandise, there has been a steady slowdown. The GST Collections of 2020-21 from the district has been only Rs 118.96 crores as against collection of Rs 133.84 crore for Koraput, Rs 178.74 crore for Rayagada;

Rs 150.11 crore for Dhenkanal, leaving aside many more areas of the state reporting much higher collections like Paradip (Rs 532.76 crores) and Jajpur (Rs 426.95 crores). This is an indicator of the prevailing moderate industrial and high-value commercial activities in the district.

The Gopalpur Steel project could not takeoff. Land acquired for the project remained unutilised for years. The land was subsequently converted to an industrial park. The Park enjoys multi-modal logistics advantage with Rail, Road and Port connectivity; it also has access to a significant export catchment comprising East-Asian countries. Gopalpur SEZ has adequate availability of skilled manpower with the presence of ITI, technical and skill development institutes in the district. Besides generating substantial employment opportunities, Gopalpur Industrial Park could contribute to the all-round socio-economic development of the region. Despite these obvious advantages, industries have been rather shy of the area. In the meantime, however, a ferro-chrome plant has come up at Gopalpur. It is the first greenfield ferro-chrome unit of Tata Steel in India. A Tea packaging unit of the Tata Group has also come up recently in the Industrial Park. More Industries should come early.

Air connectivity would help. If there are serious impediments to making the Rangeilunda air-strip a dependable facility, an alternative site needs to be selected immediately. About 1000 acres of land within a radius of 50 kms of the city would serve the purpose. The city must have a functional airport within two years with air connections with cities like Hyderabad, Bangalore, Chennai, Delhi and Mumbai. Possibility of running regular passenger ships from/to Gopalpur- Kolkata, Gopalpur-Port Blair and, if possible, Gopalpur-Yangon should be explored. Government needs to facilitate setting up of for a few

Corporate Hospitals—a critical need for the region. The city needs to improve its housing stock. This could be possible through participation of renowned real estate developers. A land bank, to start with, of 1000 acres, seems necessary where modern residential units, schools, hospitals and hotels could come up.

There is great scope for non-polluting industries including software industries in the area. The Blue waters of Tampara, the Chilka Lake and exquisitely charming beaches up to the state's border, provide huge space and opportunities for new hotels and recreational tourism. Berhampur needs a Railway Terminal facility as well. This will enable Trains to originate and terminate at the city. This would substantially improve connectivity with important Indian cities. For improving marketing opportunities for local products, dedicated e-marketing platforms need to be developed.

Civil society has to play a proactive role in unlocking the huge potential of the Silk City through a representative forum which should chalk out a blueprint for a holistic development of the city and work towards its early realisation.

Sharecroppers of Odisha

While Odisha's continuing lacklustre performance in agriculture has been due to many reasons, growing disinclination of a large number of landowners to cultivate their own lands is a major contributing factor. In some cases, the holding is too big for the owner to take care, in many cases; the owner is away from the land with another vocation on hand. These landholders have two choices -- keep the land fallow or let the needy step in on a mutually acceptable arrangement. With limited job opportunities in Odisha, the number of agriculture labourers is growing exponentially and is around 67 lakhs as against 47 lakh owner-farmers. The situation is poised against the weaker partner. These persons who cultivate others' lands with the consent of the owners settle for terms that are even inadequate for subsistence. The prevailing law is against such arrangement but deviation is rampant.

These sharecroppers — Bhagachashis — operate under heavy odds and are unable to take a long-term view about farming in the land they till. They have no access to institutional credit, both short and long-term, to meet the needs of farming. They are bereft of security of the land they till; they cannot even participate in the MSP operation and get support price for their produce. The landowners are reluctant to be magnanimous and don't disclose lease arrangement to concerned authorities. Consequently, the number of sharecroppers in government surveys doesn't capture the real situation and Odisha's ubiquitous Bhagachashi appears as a dwindling species. In fact, an official report points out that the number of sharecroppers has come down from 7.85 lakhs in 200-01 to only 5.48 lakh in 2010-11. By and large, the landless labourers and marginal farmers have accepted the sharecropping arrangement in large number and their number could be at least three times the number shown in official records. Since these close to two million sharecroppers of the state are unable to induct capital to farming, the yield remains low. Today Odisha's Bhagachashi, officially believed to be a dwindling tribe, is in the midst of a crisis of identity.

There is no level playing field for the sharecroppers so far as marketing opportunity is concerned. MSP operation for paddy provides good insurance against distress sale; but since the sharecropper won't be able to provide necessary documents to prove that he grew the paddy legitimately; his produce won't qualify for sale under MSP. Of course, the position is improving slowly and some sharecroppers are able to procure desired documents and offering their paddy at support price. Their number, however, remains modest while the vast majority of Bhagachashis sell the produce at the dictates of wily merchants.

Institutional finance has been eluding the Bhagachashis primarily because they lack worthwhile assets. The state government launched a well-drafted Bhoomihina (landless) Agriculturist Loan and Resources Augmentation Model called BALARAM Yojana. Officials outlined Government's plan to extend crop loan to 7 lakh landless sharecroppers through around 1.40 lakh Joint Liability Groups (JLGs) in two years. Since there are about 7000 Bank retail outlets in the state including Primary Credit Cooperative Societies,

Bureaucrats hoped each outlet could finance 10 farm loans and meet the target. The report of the State Level Bankers Committee however indicated that out of the total target of formation of 65000 JLGs, only 8,650 JLGs had been formed, 3517 applications forwarded to Banks for sanction and only 249 cases have been sanctioned as on 09.02.2021. It is clear that so far, the government have not been able to address this vital issue of availability of credit to the sharecroppers. They continue to be at the mercy of moneylenders.

Since sharecroppers have been rendering a socially useful service they deserve security of status, satisfactory access to adequate credit; they deserve protection against natural calamity, they need an enforceable agreement with the owner of the land and should also have the right to first refusal in case the owner wants to sell the land. There have been reports of the government mulling legislation on sharecroppers. The ideal legislation would be one that ensures mutual trust between the sharecropper and the landlord and enables the sharecropper to be a meaningful partner in ensuring higher production and productivity. A tenuous bond between the two through legislation would only lead to an exploitative atmosphere.

Both Sharecroppers as well as the Landholders are at present at the crossroads. If Odisha opts for status quo, little improvement to the living and working conditions of about two million sharecroppers would accrue and the present low productivity syndrome would only continue. On the other hand, a healthy partnership arrangement through a progressive and comprehensive legislation would lead to a win-win situation and even engender entrepreneurial drive on partnership mode among the landholders.

Odisha's Bhagachashis have been children of a lesser

God. They are in waiting mode for long. Society owes them a better tomorrow. Economy too stands to gain through higher production and increased productivity through a handholding arrangement between the Landholder and the Sharecropper. A new legal arrangement is the need of the hour. That will ensure meaningful Land Reforms in Odisha.

Doubtful if Odisha would Reach Sustainable Development Goal for 2030

Organisation for Economic Co-operation and Development (OECD), in the Development Cooperation Report of 2016 termed the Sustainable Development Goals (SDGs) as the unprecedented articulation of the public interest at a global scale for all the people of the world. Ambitious SDGs were set in 2015 for 2030. Since then, countries have been reviewing progress made, identifying bottlenecks; taking action to overcome impediments and ensuring a holistic improvement of living conditions. Six years have already passed and we have now nine years to perform and reach the goal. The SDG India Index and Dashboard developed by NITI Aayog has become an important tool for SDG monitoring by the governments, both at the central and state levels.

The document displays the performance of various states on sustainable solutions to some of the biggest challenges - ranging from poverty and gender inequality to climate change. It is a guiding framework to steer development action. It puts the states in four categories – "Achiever" with score of 100; "Front Runner" with score between 65-99; "Performer" with a score between 50-64 and "Aspirant" with a score between 0-49. Odisha has emerged as Achiever in one area — Life Below Water SDG 14; Front Runner in Eight sectors; Performer in One and Aspirant in Six areas. Areas where Odisha has been found to be weakest in intervention are SDG1- Goal for "No Poverty" with score 41; SDG2—Goal for "Zero Hunger" with score 42; SDG4- Goal for "Quality Education" with score 45; SDG5— Goal for "Gender Equality" with score 46; SDG8-Goal for "Decent Work and Economic Growth" with score 48 and SDG9-Goal for "Industry, Innovation and Infrastructure with score 46. Another area of great concern is in respect of SDG16—Goal for "Peace, Justice and Strong Institutions.

A brief discussion on these areas would indicate where Odisha stands now and the distance it needs to cover to reach the 2030 Goal in those areas.

Goal 16 focuses on ending abuse, exploitation, trafficking, corruption and bribery, and on the development of accountable and transparent institutions. It is a matter of concern that the state reports 3.1 murders per lakh population as against 1.8 for Uttarakhand and 1.9 in Puduchchery—two top performers. The 2030 goal is to reduce it to one. Cognizable crimes against children per lakh population stood at an alarming high at 49.9 against 31.5 for Uttarakhand and 10.8 for Puducherry. The goal for 2030 is to reduce it to zero. Number of missing children per lakh child population was 22.4 against 14 for Uttarakhand and 10.21 for Puducherry with the 2030 goal at zero. Presently, 20.03 persons per ten lakh population fall victim to human trafficking in Odisha as against only 3.22 for Uttarakhand and zero in Puducherry. The 2030 goal is set at zero. With SDG 16 Index score at 59, Odisha, though in category of "Performer", stands at the 36th position among 37 states and UTs, above Andaman & Nicobar Islands.

As regards "No Poverty" goal, the areas of concern are the high percentage of people below poverty line and the high percentage of kutcha houses. Odisha has 32.5% people below national poverty line and 14.2% of houses are kutcha houses—the second largest (below Arunachal Pradesh). In this Index Tamilnadu with score of 80 is at the top, with percentage of people below poverty line at 11.28% and only 2.4% kutcha houses. The goal for 2030 in these critical areas is 10.96% and zero % respectively.

Odisha's Productivity of Rice continues to be low—2003.84 kg per hectare. The goal for2030 is 5322.08 kg/ha. 29.2% of children below 5 years of age are underweighted as against Kerala's 18.7% children. 2030 goal is to reduce it to 1.9%. 47.6% of pregnant women in the age group 15-49 in Odisha are anaemic as against Kerala's 22.6% with the 2030 goal at 25.2%. These critical components of SDG Index 2 dealing with "Zero Hunger" goal, contribute to assigning Odisha a modest overall score of 42. Kerala is at the top with a score of 88.

The state has a large number of schools without access to basic infrastructure like electricity and drinking water. While states like Kerala, Sikkim, Punjab, Gujarat, Goa have ensured full coverage of schools with such infrastructure, 31.29% of Odisha's school remain deficient. The 2030 goal is to ensure 100% coverage. 27.5% of people of Odisha of 15 years and above are illiterate. Odisha's overall score in this SDG Index 4 on "Quality Education" is 45 while Kerala with a score of 80 is at the top.

The issue of Gender Equality has been analysed in SGD 5. Females have been losing in the area of wage parity. Ratio of female to male wage in Odisha is 0.66 while

2030 Goal is to bring in parity. Females have been victims of crime in large number of cases. Rate of crime against women per one lakh female population is 103.5-- one of the highest in the country while India's overall position is 62.4. The 2030 Goal is to ensure zero rate. As against the 2030 Goal of women having 50% seats in Assembly, the highest representation is in Chhattisgarh with 14.44% while Odisha has only 8.9%. As regards percentage of females operated operational holdings, it is only 4.06% while the Country's figure is 13.96. The Goal of 2030 is to have the share increased to 50 %.

In the area of decent work and economic growth SGD 8 accords the top place to Himachal Pradesh with a score of 78. Labour force participation in the age group of 15-59 is 55.2% in respect of Odisha while it is 72.1% for Himachal Pradesh. The Goal for 2030 is 66.3. Present unemployment rate in the 15-59 age group in Odisha is 7.6 %. The 2030 Goal is to bring it down to 3%. While the 2030 Goal is to ensure that no wage/salaried employee in non-agriculture sector would be without social security benefit, at present 54.3% of such employee are without social security benefit in Odisha. It is indeed a matter of great concern that in the area of ease of doing business Odisha's score is zero. This area needs special attention.

SDG 9 deals with Industry, Innovation and Infrastructure. In this area Odisha's score is 46 while Gujarat at top has a score of 72. At present out of every 100 people employed in Odisha, 8.15 are engaged in manufacturing. The 2030 Goal is to enhance it to 20. The state is having a modest innovation score at 18.94 as against the country's 35.59, while the 2030 Goal is to reach 100. Number of internet subscribers per 100 population in Odisha is 44.87 as against country's 55.41. Goal of 2030 is 100. The same

Goal is also for mobile phones. The present level in the state is 76 mobile phones for 100 population.

These areas where the progress of Odisha requires much greater political, social and governance focus are too critical to be trivialised by political cacophony. There is immediate need for an appropriate ambience that makes state's children and women secure against crimes which are at present in an unacceptable degree of virulence. Productivity of Rice has to be enhanced by 150% to reach the 2030 goal. High level of malnutrition among pregnant women and children needs special package.

❑

Stampede Outside Sri Mandir

After Covid-related restrictions on entering temples were lifted, number of devotees visiting famous shrines in India has been increasing. Around sixty thousand pilgrims visit Tirumalai now in a day. Vaishno Devi, Badrinath and Kedarnath too have now many more pilgrims. Over the years, more and more pilgrims are visiting Temples. While Vaishno Devi had 13 lakh visitors in 1986, the shrine has about 80 lakh pilgrim count now. A million devotees visited Kedarnath in 2019. On 10th of June in 2019, over 36,000 visited the Temple. Sabarimala attracts 40 to 50 million devotees in a year. That Jagannath Dham Puri would attract more devotees for darshan is therefore only natural.

Of late, reports have come in about inconvenience devotees have experienced in gaining entry into the Srimandir. Visuals of thousands of devotees including children and ladies standing for hours in hot sun and waiting for their turn to get inside the temple convey a distressing picture. The line of devotees has become too long. On last Phagu Purnima the situation turned chaotic as exasperated devotees created a 'stampede' near Singhadwar (the entrance to the temple) to witness Suna Besha of Holy Trinity.

Discontentment over mismanagement is widespread

indicating a severe sensitivity deficit. Response of the administration has been inadequate and suffering of devotees seems to be open-ended. Some garden umbrellas placed at a few places, a carpet spread on the road and some bottles of water for the parched throats are baby steps and only confirm the persisting obduracy and insensitivity of people who matter.

Regulating entry of devotees -- VIPs are exceptions -- to the Temple through only one gate has been an avoidable copy and paste decision of the government which seems to have been oblivious to the size and amenities Bada-Deula (Big Temple) provides for devotees. The huge temple and the spacious circulation space inside were created by our forefathers with great far sight. For hundreds of years, devotees used all four gates of the Temple for entry and exit in most days. Devotees living nearby the South Gate preferred South Gate while devotees of Sahis (locality) close to Western Gate used that particular Gate. It is true, over years the number of pilgrims visiting Jagannath temple has risen and justified adequate regulations to be put in place. Regulatory arrangement, however, should have been in sync with age-old practices and existing facilities in the temple. What administrators did was avoidable. It led to an artificial crowding. Devotees could have been led to different gates and crowding for entry through one gate avoided. This would have meant standing under the hot sun for a considerably short period.

The present chaos looks all the more paradoxical because a hugely expensive and comprehensive programme has been taken up by the Government for regeneration of the ancient Puri. While the programme is a bold one and one of its kind in the state, it seems to have faltered badly so far as devotees' comforts are concerned. Devotees are made to stand for hours under the hot sun. There is scant respect for punctuality; temple rituals are generally delayed; Mahaprasad is seldom available on time; and even if available, has become too expensive for the common devotees.

What devotees are missing is sensitivity and empathy. The stampede-like situation on Holi Purnima seems to be a wakeup call. Devotees do deserve a lot more respect and attention and it is the bounden duty of the state government to ensure this without delay.

❑

Vandalism in the Temple Kitchen

As night grows darker, a busy day for the Lords draws to a close and the Jagannath Temple activities get oriented towards the day's last ritual for the Lords– Bada Sinhar Besha. A few devotees– maybe fifty, hang on in the vast premises of the Temple. Some bid time on the Achinta Mandap of the Temple of Goddess Laxmi, while some sing Bhajan in the glory of the Lords there, others listen. At this hour inside the main Temple, the concerned servitor hurries, carrying a basket of fragrant flowers for bedecking the Lords. Sandal-paste is applied to the Holy Trinity and the Lords don special Silk and get bedecked with garlands and flowers. It is time now for offering the sibling deities their last meal of the day before they go to bed. A small number of devotees get a glimpse of the Lords in Bada Sinhar Besha. A servitor now sings in the glory of the Lords to make the Lords sleep. The devotees still hang on to have a portion of the Bhog. Besides different types of Pithas, Bhog includes Mitha Pakhala and Kadali Bada, the taste of which is beyond description.

The magic of the Srimandir Temple Kitchen (Rosa Ghara) is unique; for centuries, servitors in charge of preparing food for the Lords have expressed their love, affection and dedication to the Living God through their culinary skill and cooked varieties of delicacies – Chhapan Bhog – for the health and happiness of the Lords.

For centuries, the Temple Kitchen has been special, both in size and in its way of cooking. It has about two hundred fifty wood-fired chulhas. Chulhas are of three kinds. While majority of them are used for cooking Rice (Anna), the rest are Pitha chulhas and Ahia–square sized, (for cooking Dal, Vegetables etc.). Chulhas are highly valuable properties. Years ago, most chulhas belonged to Mathas but gradually these were taken on lease or on transfer to Supakars. Ownership used to change from time to time and in the past an owner, in need of money, would incur a loan of a few lakhs of rupees by mortgaging a chula. Instances of ownership changing hands through verbal agreement are there. Chula continues to be bone of contention and gives rise to rivalry, jealousy and disputes among Supakar fraternity. Cooking is made for ten thousand to a hundred thousand people and therefore it is big business.

Report on Sunday (April 3, 2022) about damage to 43 chulhas the previous night took the temple town and the entire Odia fraternity by surprise. Perhaps for the first time were so many chulhas (17% of the total) reportedly vandalised. Revelations that the kitchen door had not been locked the previous night was shocking.

There were reports that temple policemen were not on duty near the entry to the kitchen. That only six out of the total 135 CCTV Cameras were in operational state revealed lackadaisical security arrangement. A person was found well after midnight inside the temple premises and was taken out of the temple by four policemen of the Jagannath Temple Police (JTP).

The claim of the police that they worked on leads

and nabbed the culprit in his village in Khordha district does not sound convincing. However, the man picked up seemed to have admitted to have damaged the chulhas singlehandedly without even any tool like a crowbar. He reportedly reacted on the spur of the moment after entering the kitchen as he felt disturbed over commercialisation of Mahaprasad. This version, however, has few buyers. It is widely believed that vandalism on such a wide scale could not have been possible by a lone perpetrator. It is more probable that the act was premeditated and perpetrated by a few people to settle scores.

The incident raises a few important issues involving security of the temple and management of Mahaprasad. These issues are not new; these have been persisting and kept under carpet despite increasing presence of Government inside the Temple. This is worrisome. Government seems more engaged in an expensive facelift of the surroundings of the Temple. A casual attitude to pilgrims' difficulties has not helped.

While the act of vandalism in the temple kitchen does warrant an in-depth investigation instead of a swift closure of the case following the arrest of one man and his statement, Government must fix responsibility on persons responsible for severe security lapses detected after the incident. It is inconceivable that in a highly sensitive place like the Jagannath Temple almost all the CCTV cameras would be dysfunctional. It is also important that management of Mahaprasad is efficiently organised to again make Mahaprasad an integral part of the Divine experience a devotee always aspired for.

❑

Tsunami of Freebies before Polls

For the recently held Odisha Panchayat Election, the electoral roll comprised 2.79 crore rural voters. Election was held to elect 91,913 Ward Members, 6,794 Sarpanches, 6,793 Panchayat Samiti Members and 853 Zilla Parishad members. Detailed guidelines for a Covid-safe election was issued that said that there would be no road shows, padayatra, cycle/bike/vehicle rally or procession. No physical rally of political parties or probable candidates or any other group related to election was to be allowed. Only door-to-door campaign with participation of maximum five people including the candidate was allowed. The poll panel had also advised the political parties and candidates to conduct their campaigns as much as possible through digital, virtual, media platforms and mobile-based modes. Model code of conduct came into effect on time and this remained in force till the completion of counting of votes i.e. February 28.

While the country was in the grip of revival of Covid cases, and Odisha being no exception, there was speculation on whether the election would be deferred. Hon'ble High Court however rejected a prayer for deferring the Election.

Government kept on showering their favours to different segments of the voters ranging from Anganwadi workers to over aged aspirants for government jobs. Some favours costing hundreds of crores of rupees to the state exchequer kept rolling out of Naveen Government's gift box without even a demand for it. One such favour merits a discussion.

Biju Pucca Ghar Yojana is a state plan scheme introduced in 2014 to give effect to the state government's commitment to provide pucca houses to all the rural households living in kutcha houses. The detailed government guidelines on the subject issued in 2017 superseding earlier instructions made it clear that the expected life of the structure must be a minimum of thirty years. Strangely, however, the government decided to give Rs 3000 to beneficiaries to repair their houses allotted to them under the Biju Pucca Ghar Yojana. No one had asked for it; nor was it known why Rs 3000 would be the right amount. Government also announced that those who have not yet availed houses under the Pradhan Mantri Awas Yojana (PMAY) would get Rs 5000 to carry out repairs of the houses. Nearly 30 lakh people would benefit from the announcement. Around Rs 1,444 crore could have been spent in this regard. All the money was to be credited to the bank accounts of the beneficiaries directly.

Some of the decisions taken immediately before the Election announcement transcended logic. One case was about making over aged aspirants eligible for government jobs. In some cases, even a 53-year-old person was made eligible for a government job. It was clarified that since the recruitment process got held up for two years due to the unprecedented situation arising out of the pandemic, age relaxation was considered necessary. But the 5-years age relaxation to compensate recruitment held up for two years is difficult to understand. That this concession was valid for only three years makes it looked really clumsy.

The last session of the Legislative Assembly closed days before the schedule. The Chief Minister did not attend the Assembly though he appeared in the Kalinga Stadium for a Sports event and, soon after the sine die adjournment of the Assembly, chose to visit a few districts to distribute the Biju Swasthya Kalyan Yojana (BSKY) smart cards to beneficiaries.

The Naveen era has been in the state for over two decades. The party led by Naveen Patnaik has fought many elections and has won decisively. Against this backdrop, why was the run up to the Panchayat Election marked by a tsunami of financial concessions and favours costing the government thousands of crores of rupees, raises the issue of political morality – enticing voters through government largesse and diverting huge chunks of government resource for winning elections.

A developed State after 22 years of rule by Naveen Patnaik would have been an appropriate Naveen legacy; but unfortunately even now, the state government has identified as many as 96.5 lakh families (out of a total of 97.5 lakh families in the state) under the Biju Swasthya Kalyan Yojana as economically vulnerable families and about 55 lakh families are getting one rupee rice for being poor. Reckless spending of taxpayers' money on freebies could win elections, but does not bring in holistic development of the state. Liberal use of Freebies to win Elections looks an anachronism at this stage of the Naveen era. This political strategy is not what statesmanship should be about.

❑

Biju Swasthya Kalyan Yojana – an Analysis

Odisha continues with a modest health infrastructure. With 2501 hospitals including 695 in private sector, the state provides only 25,650 hospital beds as against Kerala's 3342 hospitals including 2062 private hospitals providing 99,227 hospital beds— almost four times. Odisha's hospitals have 1282 ICU Beds and 641 ventilators while Kerala provided 4961 ICU Beds and 2481 ventilators. While private sector is the dominant provider of hospital beds, ICU and ventilator facilities in Kerala; public sector is the dominant provider in Odisha.

Most of India's hospital beds and ventilators are concentrated in seven States - Uttar Pradesh (14.8%), Karnataka (13.8%), Maharashtra (12.2%), Tamil Nadu (8.1%), West Bengal (5.9%), Telangana (5.2%) and Kerala (5.2%). Private sector has dominant presence in India's health facilities having more hospitals, more hospital beds, more ICUs and more ventilators than what the public sector hospitals have.

Since over 80% of Indians were without health insurance cover, high hospitalisation charges were paid by people out of their savings or borrowing. The Ayushman Bharat initiative of Government of India covering about 11 crore poor families of the country came as a great relief to the economically vulnerable people as hospitalisation was made free for them up to a reasonable financial limit. Odisha Government, however, decided to launch its own scheme and crafted an Assurance scheme making about 99% of the state's families eligible for cashless treatment facilities in empanelled private hospitals for some ailments.

Biju Swasthya Kalyan Yojana (BSKY) has been launched, as the state government says, as a "path-breaking programme" to provide universal health coverage, with special emphasis on the health protection of economically vulnerable families. The goal is sought to be achieved through two components. First one is the State Government will bear full cost of all health services delivered to all patients (irrespective of income, status or residence) in all State Government health care facilities starting from sub-centre level to district headquarters and Government Medical College Hospital and Blood Bank level. Second, the State Government will bear the cost of healthcare provided in empanelled private hospitals for over 96.5 lakh economically vulnerable families in the State, amounting to Annual Health coverage of Rs 5 lakh per family and Rs 5 lakh for the women members of the family over and above the five-lakh limit.

Two areas in this scheme, however, need a closer look. The state's population in 2021 is estimated at 46.8 million. The average size of a family in India is 4.8. On this basis, the state would have a total number of 97.5 lakh families. The state government has covered as many as 96.5 lakh families under the BSKY identifying them as economically vulnerable families. This leaves only one lakh families of the state who seem to be economically well off. This is a sad commentary on the quality of implementation of the poverty amelioration programmes of the state government for over two decades. The second area of concern is the policy to provide everyone free medical facility, medicines, in government health institutions. Here both the poor and the rich benefit. If this is the case, why then are hundreds of medicine shops functioning, why are there so many diagnostic centres, and where is the requirement of so many private medical professionals in the state? Obviously, they are in business because they have customers. Private hospitals too remain overcrowded. This raises issues of credibility and quality of service.

Official website mentions that since its inception on August 15, 2018, the BSKY has launched a new era in Universal Health Coverage, with over 45 lakh instances of cashless treatment being provided each month. The scheme is being operated by the State Health Assurance Society. As per the arrangement, the private hospitals are to submit claims within a month and the valid claims would be paid by the government within two months. Reports, however, have started appearing in the press about pending claims of private hospitals and about the cost of treatment fixed by the government being unrealistically low and unworkable. The scheme, it appears, has hit road-blocks soon after being in operation. It is apprehended that with the number of smart-card holders seeking treatment in empanelled hospitals increasing, timely payment of claims by the Assurance Society would pose real problem leading to disruption of cashless facility—a situation encountered by many beneficiaries of the Central Government Health Scheme (CGHS) in Odisha in respect of many empanelled hospitals in Bhubaneswar.

To realise the Chief Minister's faith that "every life is precious" the state must have adequate number of Doctors, Nurses, paramedical staff, adequate and functional equipment. The state however is acutely short of doctors; the infrastructure is just modest; cases of ambulance failing to reach waiting patients in time are many. These areas of concern warrant much greater attention.

Chief Minister touring various districts for distribution of the smart cards for the BSKY immediately after the last Assembly session (which he did not attend) was adjourned much before the schedule makes many wonder if it was intended to garner political dividends in the impending elections to the ULBs and PRIs. Many also feel that the reason for keeping the state away from the national scheme of Ayushman Bharat was to generate political support. But it needs to be appreciated that our system of government is a party based arrangement and a party in power is well within its rights to shape policies that ensure both public good and beneficial for the party. In that sense, the BSKY is a bold political initiative but a hugely expensive and challenging one. And in the context of the Ayushman Bharat initiative of Government of India it could look to be an avoidable adventure. Today it looks highly susceptible to hitting roadblocks. It will be a pity if it doesn't succeed. For its success, the state needs a robust infrastructure which it now doesn't have.

❑

Need for Legal Literacy

Despite exponential spread of literacy in the country after India attained Independence, it is a matter of concern that our people, by and large, continue to be in a state of legal illiteracy. A piece of legislation is passed by the legislature; public discussion on it or its features are seldom held. After the Bill gets the assent of the President or Governor, it is published in the official gazette for public knowledge. This is no more than a mere formality. People, by and large, remain totally indifferent. We are now in a situation where we do not know the law but are subject to it. Very often we are made aware of the law only after we have violated it. Legal illiteracy has facilitated both highhandedness of public servants and illegal activities in the society.

National Legal Services Authority does undertake various awareness activities to make people aware of their rights and about the role, activities and functioning of the legal services institutions. Though a variety of tools are used to achieve this objective, outcome has been extremely limited and legal awareness continues to be poor.

The situation gets further chaotic when the law enforcement authority too is not conversant with the law it is mandated to implement. As a result, we get into a situation where there is abundance of law but understanding of it remains confined to the lawyers and the judges. This situation in effect leads to de facto rule of men rather than rule of law.

Recently, citizens of Bhubaneswar experienced a similar situation when Bhubaneswar Municipal Corporation "revised" the Holding Tax, Latrine Tax and Lighting Tax with effect from 2019-20 and made many denizens pay hefty amounts even though the whole exercise lacked legal sanction. Most citizens were unaware of the law. Even very senior citizens who occupied senior position in government fell victim.

For instance, a close friend, Bijay Kumar Mohanty, a former senior officer of the Cooperation Department, who used to pay only Rs 540/- as Holding Tax, Latrine Tax and Lighting Tax and paid this amount also for 2019-20, found his tax "revised" from 2019-20 to Rs 7044/- per year and he was asked to pay Rs. 13,520/ for two years. He did. When I asked him why he did, he said he was a law-abiding citizen and did not think that an official would ever make a demand if it wasn't an authorised one.

Another friend, Gopal Mohanty who retired from a post equivalent to Special Secretary to the state Government, also paid, disregarding my advice not to pay the revised tax as the revision was not authorized by law. Not only these two, hundreds of citizens, including an Hon'ble Member of Parliament and his father, paid whatever was asked for by the Bhubaneswar Municipal Corporation. A few of us did whatever was possible– to reach out to friends and relatives, advising them not to pay and explained the position of law. I even appealed to political parties in my Tweet to intervene. These efforts did not make a difference.

Somehow, Opposition Parties came in. Government suddenly responded, stopped further collection of the Holding Tax at the revised rate and awaited Court Orders.

It was a relief to those who had not paid. What was, however, surprising was Government didn't examine the issue of the legality of the revision. There was complete lack of understanding of the provisions of the Municipal Corporation Act.

The matter was finally decided by Hon'ble Orissa High Court on April 22, 2021, in Kalyani Maternity Hospital Pvt. Ltd., Bhubaneswar versus Bhubaneswar Municipal Corporation. Hon'ble High Court held that Bhubaneswar Municipal Corporation (BMC) was competent to collect tax which was leviable immediately before commencement of the Municipal Corporation (OMC) Act. The law by no means permitted BMC to levy any fresh tax after the enactment of the OMC Act under the transitional provisions of the Act. Fresh tax had to be levied only under the substantive provisions of the Municipal Corporation Act. Under the Municipal Corporation Act, there was no place for Holding Tax. The Court held that the demand notice of the BMC seeking collection of the revised holding tax from the Petitioner for a period after the commencement of the OMC Act, and at a rate higher than that was prevalent when the Odisha Municipality Act was in force, was unsustainable in law. The demand notice was therefore quashed.

Here was a case where officers responsible for the execution of a law and most citizens were in dark about the relevant provisions of law in question. That this indefensible situation prevailed in the capital city of the state and the denizens of the city, mostly highly educated, fell victim to ignorance of law, is an indicator of the pervading lack of awareness about the contents of various laws both by the citizenry and the officials mandated to enforce them.

We must work towards improvement of legal literacy in Odisha. A welfare State should be eager to have a proactive role in this effort. We have a Department of Government that looks after Public Grievance. Role of this Department could be recast and legal literacy drive initiated through assistance of eminent people in legal profession and social activists. Officials of the state government too should have regular refreshers course to make them more conversant and knowledgeable on various legislations in force.

❑

Transforming Odisha Schools

By the turn of the 20th century, Odisha had a few High Schools. Zila School at Cuttack started in 1851. Balasore and Puri Zila Schools were established in 1853, while Sambalpur Zila School started functioning in 1858. Deogarh had the High School in 1882, Paralakhemundi, in 1875 and Baripada, in 1889. By now, there are about 4630 Government High Schools in the state and account for about 60% of the total number of High Schools of the state. Shortage of teaching staff is now a chronic problem with the Government High Schools. As on November 23, 2020, over a thousand Government High Schools went without Headmasters.

Litigations have led to abnormal delay in deployment of Headmasters and litigations do not end soon. Credible political concern is seldom noticed over this serious issue. Shortage of Trained Graduate Teachers in critical disciplines like Computer, Science makes the Government High Schools increasingly less popular and useful. Parents and students prefer to shift to private schools, mostly those which teach in English medium.

Government, of late, however, seems to be active on a reform agenda. Adarsh Vidyalaya, Model School, is one initiative worth mentioning. It is a watershed in the sense that these State Government High Schools would provide a unique opportunity to meritorious students of rural Odisha all facilities available in expensive private schools. When fully developed, these 314 schools would offer over 25,000 students every year for the school final examination. These schools have adopted CBSE syllabus and English is the medium of instruction. Basically, Adarsha Vidyalayas have infrastructure and facilities of the standard available in Kendriya Vidyalaya in critical areas like Pupil-Teacher ratio, ICT usages, holistic educational environment and appropriate curriculum. The unit cost of first phase buildings was Rs 3 crore; now each unit costs around Rs 5 crore. These Vidyalayas have adequate ICT infrastructure and internet connectivity with sufficient scope for sports and co-curricular activities. The reservation of seats for students is as per the percentage of SC & ST population in the respective Blocks and half of the students have to be girls. So far, 214 Adarsha Vidyalayas have been made operational in 29 districts and 30 schools have been upgraded to Higher Secondary level.

The result of the first batch in 100 schools, however, has not been encouraging. Out of 5981 students who appeared in CBSE Examination, 1055 students (18%) failed. Only 5.6% of students secured 90% or above and 30% secured 75% and above. The result is surely a wakeup call to the government and once again proves that expensive infrastructure alone doesn't ensure a good school. Quality of teaching is an area that needs closer monitoring to ensure that this initiative of the government becomes a success.

Odisha continues with its efforts towards transformation of schools and kick-started the smart classroom project recently. For reasons best known to government, it chose to cover 50 Government High Schools of Hinjli Assembly Constituency comprising Hinjili and Shergad Blocks reportedly spending Rs 45 lakh per school. Each school has smart classroom, e-library cum reading room, modern science laboratory, hygienic toilets and adequate sports infrastructure. These projects are stated to have been undertaken under state government's 5T (Technology, Teamwork, Time, Transparency & Transformation) initiative.

Hinjli is the Constituency of the Chief Minister and perhaps that was the reason why fifty schools in his constituency were handpicked for the programme ignoring ancient schools of the state which have been serving the community for over 150 years and where perhaps there was much greater chance of success of the programme. Soon after Shergad Block got 27 high schools converted to smart high schools, students and guardians noticed the absence of IT teachers. For some days, classes are being somehow managed. Teachers with working knowledge of computers are running the systems. A few years ago, computer teachers had been engaged in some schools in this Block through a contractual agency to impart computer education. But those teachers were disengaged. Computers worth lakhs of rupees are gathering dust in closed rooms. In Kumuli High School in Boriguma Block of Koraput District, smart classroom was started for which Block administration spent Rs 5 lakhs and through convergence of resources of various schemes. The district is planning to cover one school per Block for its 14 Blocks.

Odisha plans to transform in the first phase 1,070 schools with modern facilities and Government feels that the move would lay the foundation for a progressive Odisha. Chief Minister said the decision to transform the schools will bring new opportunities for children of the state and will help them fulfil their dreams.

Smart classrooms are expected to improve students' learning abilities through integration of technology in and outside the classroom. By integrating technology, we could make students stay engaged in classroom as interactive modules like videos and presentations would make teaching appealing to students who hitherto have been struggling with the traditional method of teaching in a classroom. Through audio-visual presentations, students will access new frontiers of knowledge by travelling throughout the world from virtual platform. To take full advantage of this new facility, students need mentors in capable teachers. This needs to be ensured. The stock of teachers the state has may not assimilate new technology in the same manner or same speed. Some could be fast learners while many would be slow or remain indifferent like one of my colleagues and good friend who, despite my efforts, couldn't learn to operate his email account.

The strategy Odisha has adopted to replace school blackboard by smart-board is rather unconventional. Schools have not gone through an objective and strenuous screening process to win a smart classroom as has been the case in Srinagar. Here a school has been selected merely because it is located in the constituency of the VVIP. The school has been a beneficiary of a paternalistic favour; it has not earned it. The case of the school in Boriguma Block in Koraput shows it has gone for a less elaborate infrastructure than a school in Hinjili or Shergad.

Odisha needs to address the important issue of modality of selection of schools, uniformity in infrastructure facility, and above all, must ensure availability of qualified teachers in schools. A massive expensive building with state of art toilet, a swanky swimming pool and a gym without a Headmaster or adequate number of qualified teachers does not create a smart school.

Government of India has planned to provide by March 2023, two smart classrooms in all 1,01,967 Government and 42,917 Aided schools in all States/UTs and 1704 KVs and NVs making a total of 1,46,588 schools. Thereby there would be a switch to digital boards from blackboards in every school in the country in a phased manner. Odisha would do well to dovetail its programme into the national plan.

◻

Odisha School Education
at a Crossroads

A video clip is doing rounds on social media showing a spirited youth asking how learning the formula of (A+B) whole square would equip him in life; how it would make his life easier in grocery shop or while buying vegetables or how it would help him in married life or how well off it would make him when he becomes a father. If the formula was not of any help in these situations, why, he was asking with anger and emotion, was he being asked by his teacher in the school to remember. The satire and his anger did not appear totally irrelevant. He represents a huge number of students in the tribal sub-plan area of Odisha where schooling in its present state has limited appeal. Media men have reported their experience of students demonstrating huge academic deficits where students studying in class seven or eight would not be able to count numbers if you asked them to count numbers, say, between 17 and 94. Students in class eight or nine would not be able to say what the whole square of A+B is equal to. For many students, a government school does not open any new world of opportunities nor does the quality of teaching, the environment of the school or available facilities sustain the interest of most students.

State of school education in Odisha continues to

remain a matter of serious concern. The sector is afflicted with problems like serious shortage of teachers and severe deficit in infrastructure. These deficiencies are more acute in underdeveloped regions of the state.

Given the quality of teaching in the remote areas of the tribal region of the state, the bond of the average student with the school has always been tenuous. The teacher has rarely been able to ignite his imagination; study has mostly been uninteresting – little beyond a rote learning exercise, without any "connect" with the vast ocean of knowledge. The teacher, by and large, has been a disgruntled person with a heavy baggage of grievance. He is rarely supervised; never held in respect, supervisors have seldom been accountable. The school ambience offered little to cheer about.

Whatever link the school offered to a student of average merit, however, abruptly snapped when it closed indefinitely following the pandemic.

It was too facile an assumption that on reopening of the schools after almost two academic years, students in the remote areas would rush to the schools, particularly where schooling was never an attractive and lovable experience for the students. Teachers were always in shortage; many were engaged on contract and underpaid. Thousands of students hardly understood what was taught, there was little pressure from parents, mostly illiterate, to study at home. In many cases young hands in school meant loss of wage earning opportunity for a poor family; in many cases migration for work to a distant place was much more convenient if the young children too accompanied the parents.

Long closure of schools due to the pandemic

facilitated engagement of the young children in wage earning activities; wherever they remained idle they became vulnerable to enticement of extremists looking for young recruits. Government mandarins, mostly operating in ivory towers, presumed that the online coaching would keep students occupied in study. Severe constraints on appropriate infrastructure made participation in online teaching extremely difficult. Bulk of the students was unable to take advantage of online teaching. As a result, most of them forgot what they had learnt and about 18 lakh students did not return to schools when schools reopened. Where the Government blundered was it did not ensure that the teachers remained in regular touch with the students even when the schools remained closed.

Shortage of teachers has been a chronic problem in the state and more acute in the outlying regions of the state. Many teachers do not enjoy the regular pay scale and remain engaged on contract. They live in a state of perpetual discontentment. A teacher's availability for teaching is getting limited. He is either engaged in election duties or pulse polio campaigns or maintaining mid-day meal registers. A report released by the National Institute of Education and Administration (NUEPA) disclosed that only 19.1 percent of a teacher's annual school hours was spent on teaching activities. The remaining part of the teacher's time devoted to non-teaching core activities (42.6%), to non-teaching school related activities (31.8%) and to other department activities (6.5%). Lack of supervision has resulted in a high degree of teacher-absenteeism.

Poor infrastructure has been endemic for the rural schools in Odisha. Out of 50,256 government schools, 15663 (31.17%) did not have electricity facilities as per the Report on 2020-21 of Unified District Information System for

Education Plus (UDISE+) of the Government of India. The rest, though with functional electricity facilities, suffered long hours of power outage. In 2019-20, only 10.61% of government schools had medical checkup of students. This was the lowest in the country. Only 14.25% of Odisha's government schools offered functional computer facilities as against the national average of 31.11%. While 3,21,024 government schools in the country had functional computer facility it is interesting to note that Chhattisgarh provided functional computer facility in 40,014 government schools, Maharashtra to 40607, Jharkhand to 29651, Tamil Nadu to 29,732 and Odisha to only 7162 government schools. Out of a total of 10,32,049 government schools in the country, 140745 (13.64 %) schools had Internet facilities. Gujarat offered this facility in 25301 schools, Jharkhand to 10334 schools, Punjab to 19260 schools, Rajasthan to 19255 schools, Chhattisgarh to 4116 schools while Odisha offered only to 1428 government schools (which accounts for 2.84%). Almost every government school in Delhi, Gujarat, Kerala and Punjab has by now Internet facilities.

Prevailing lackadaisical attitude over two decades to the all important sector of school education has resulted in severe erosion of credibility of schooling with a large segment of population in underdeveloped areas of the state. The Odisha Board of Secondary Education (BSE) reporting that 43,489 students had skipped out on the 10th Exams in 2022 is an indication of the critical situation.

Again, as many as 14,935 students in Odisha did not appear in the Class 9 (2021-22) examination, though they were among the 5,66,269 students who had enrolled for the Class 9 examination. And now the most vivid revelation of widespread disillusionment has come with 30% of the school students not returning to schools post pandemic.

The state government, of course, has launched a flagship "Mo School" programme for modernising schools and some school premises now wear a new look. But the programme would be successful if it addressed the core. Large number of hostels has also been established for the benefit of thousands of tribal students. Obviously, these initiatives have fallen short in ensuring a meaningful transformation. Clearly, Odisha's school education sector is passing through a critical phase that warrants much more than an easy shortcut approach.

Revival of the school in the far-flung area needs a meaningful reappraisal of the role of the school teacher. In any reform for improving schooling, the school must have amenities like electricity, computer and internet. At the same time, the teacher must get back his/her dignity and be provided with necessary wherewithal to make learning much more interesting and meaningful for the students.

☐

Rejuvenating Bhubaneswar City

The heritage corridor around Shree Jagannath Temple in Puri may be viewed as Odisha's Signature Project on urban regeneration. This breakthrough makes me hopeful that such initiatives are possible in other places as well. So many towns and cities in Odisha are in need of improvement. While it is understandable that ancient urban centres like Cuttack and Puri would need urgent interventions to make them more livable, we need to be equally sensitive to the fast deterioration of urban infrastructures even in not-so-old towns and cities. Bhubaneswar is a unique amalgam of the ancient and modern. Both segments of the city have areas of concern and need addressing. In this piece I write in some details about Bhubaneswar.

By and large there has been a soft attitude to the growing urban aberrations like footpaths becoming inaccessible to pedestrians; markets becoming centres of chaos and unauthorised structures mushrooming all over the city. Such aberrations have steadily grown in magnitude and made city life increasingly unhygienic and unsafe. While these areas of concern keep growing and need effective intervention with adequate investments, there are instances where huge public expenditure has been made on projects which were either avoidable or of marginal benefit to the public. The expensive Raj Mahal Flyover with a faulty orientation that finally emerged after cost and time overrun, serves little purpose. So also, is the elaborate pedestrian over bridge at Pal Heights Hotel that looks to me as the most expensive Bill Board ever built by any Municipal Corporation in India. In contrast, a credible Bus Terminal is yet to come up in the city.

The oldest Daily Market in the capital city that even sixty years ago hosted a well-designed mutton sale counter where slain goat bodies always showed quality verification marks of the Health Officer is a complete shambles. The walled Daily Market and its surroundings extending to beautiful government quarters at the back, is a textbook example of urban chaos, squalor and years of government indifference. The place continues to remain highly vulnerable to fire hazard as well. The place where we have the plaque on the foundation of the New Capital suffers as a sore spot. The surroundings of the historic and beautiful building known as Sardar Patel Hall, where Odisha Legislative Assembly had functioned, has now degenerated with filth and shanties in abundance. A time-bound programme on priority basis should be taken up to redevelop these areas to appropriate standard.

Huge amount of public money has been liberally spent in a few new government office buildings without any benefit to the denizens of the city. This resource perhaps had better claimants like a Bus Terminal or Hospitals or new modern markets. Conditions around the city's main Railway Station remain awfully disorganised. Public Tanks in the city, so essential for a city prone to cyclones when electricity supply remains disrupted for days, do not inspire confidence. Even the legendary Kedar Gouri Tank is in an utter state of neglect. These assets need immediate renovation for serving the needs of the community.

The city, now home to barely 1.2 million people, seems to be afflicted with premature ageing, primarily due to government apathy. Many arterial roads have proved inadequate to growing traffic soon after construction. The city has been rather unkind to the pedestrians and cyclists. Public spaces are shrinking due to increasing caprice and deficient enforcement. The malady is still remediable provided we address these issues with sensitivity and alacrity.

The city also needs to have a workable futuristic plan for long term sustainability. The city is richly endowed with water resources with Kuakhai and Daya Rivers flowing close by. Both the Rivers must have River Front Development programmes drawing from the experience of the Sabarmati project. In the case of the Sabarmati project, average width of the river channel was uniformly narrowed to 263 metres without affecting its flood-carrying capacity and the riverbed land reclaimed on both banks was used to construct long riverfront. It improved the environment by reducing erosion of the banks and flooding of low-lying areas of the city by walls constructed on both banks. The development enabled groundwater recharge. The Project boasts of a Lotus Lake, Riverfront Flower Park, an Urban Forest. Such projects for Bhubaneswar would make the city a lot more livable and save both Rivers from ongoing unbridled defilement.

Lakhs of people rendering essential services in the city but economically weak, have preferred to live in shanties spread over large areas in many parts of the city. There is an understandable preference of such people to live close to downtown. The solution to this issue lies in having Condominia, with each Condominium housing hundreds of Apartments for such people.

Bhubaneswar enjoys a wide reputation as a greatly livable Indian city with amiable people, soothing afternoon breeze, tasty drinking water and satisfactory air, road and rail connectivity. The city should grow to greater heights as a more planned city with cleaner roads, cleaner marketplaces and healthy public space. We should plan for a two million city with appropriate development of satellite towns at Jatni, Khurda, Barang and Pahala with healthy integration with the main city. We can ill afford to delay the regeneration programme. A soft approach to degeneration has snowballed to a situation where the capital city's Raj Path has become almost impassable having been converted into a marketplace. We need to guard against the city turning wholesale into a Bazaar and lose its unique identity.

A Visit of my Friend

We met this morning after many months. He looked healthier and cheerful. Years ago, he was a valued colleague. He used to read and write regularly on the subject he was associated with for long while he was a senior official in government. He now finds pleasure reading on homeopathy and occasionally visiting his Master's ashram and meditating before His Samadhi. He spoke to me about the protracted litigation over his pension. He feels he is entitled to higher amount than what has been sanctioned. The matter concerns a number of retired officers as well; but he has been at the forefront, studying the issue, preparing the plaint, briefing the lawyer, spending his money. While we were talking, he received a call. He spoke to the caller briefly and said he would talk to him after an hour. The caller was yet another colleague-- equally bright, knowledgeable and broad-minded. He was in an important assignment before he retired. On the day he retired he was put under a disciplinary proceeding that caused him considerable anguish. He fought till the end and got justice. By then he was a sick man. The genial smile that was the hallmark of his persona had gone forever. He now takes short walks, that too with the support of a stick. We remembered yet another bright officer who faced turbulence in professional life in the last phase of his career. He was of nobler and softer stuff; he soon wilted and recently passed away. Unwittingly, we had an overview of the universe we lived in. It has been an arena not free from jealousy, cruelty and intrigue. Both the cases we discussed had originated from intrigue and jealousy. The eco system remains prone to arrogance and even penalises rectitude and professionalism. The victim soon becomes lonely; he fights alone, against a mighty adversary. In such a situation, rate of casualty, inevitably is high.

It was time for him to leave. I went up to his car. A smart and respectful youth had driven him to our house. He is a fresh engineering graduate. My friend had told me about him. He is the elder of the two sons of a person who along with his wife has been looking after my friend and his wife all these years and they lived in the friend's household. I advised the boy to prepare for a government job through the Public Service Commission. He agreed. I knew I was prompting him to a sector where all was not well. But then, considering the financial situation his family was in, I would not have done the right thing suggesting that he spent time and money in a mega city, looking for a job at a time when majority of the engineering pass-outs are considered unemployable.

☐

The Disillusioned Oldman

What I am writing now is about a person my friend, Gopal, knew rather well. He had spoken about his plights some years ago while both of us walked in the morning in the Temple Garden. Gopal had pleaded that I should write about it so that families drew lesson from it and lived a normal life. This is how Gopal had told me the story.

"He didn't mind doing errands on the request of the son and the son's wife. He loved both of them. Their chubby two-year-old son was the apple of his eyes. He had retired from a very high position in the government and therefore had reasonable saving and earned a handsome pension. He was not short of money. He didn't mind spending his money to run the house though his son too was on a good job and was earning well.

In the beginning, the errands were occasional for some time but not before long had become a daily ritual. Every morning his dear son's wife would give him a chit having a score of items-- ranging from toothpicks to detergent powder-- written on it and he was expected to go to the market, buy the items from the department store and then roam around looking for fresh brinjal, tender Bhindi etc as per the specifications spelt out to him by her verbally.

The elderly loving man soon felt slighted at the

daily command, he was now greatly disillusioned and an otherwise agreeable household-chore soon turned into a drudgery. It hurt his self-esteem. He felt he was losing his stature and was turning into a beast of burden. His lonely existence after the passing away of his wife had become more oppressive.

One day he quietly left his house, reached an old age home in the city and stayed on. Life was less taunting. But the innocent smile of the child at home kept haunting him. An urge swelled within and made him restive, pushing him to go back to the child who too loved him. Living now in the old age home looked desolate; the music had stopped.

One day he reached the tea stall close to his house in the morning and waited for his son to pass that way on his way to the office. The son did come that way; he saw the father but didn't stop to take him home, to his grandchild as the grandfather had hoped for.

He felt suddenly strong, stood up, wiped his eyes and walked away from the tea shop. He reached the old age home, leaving emotions behind.

□

Bhaat and Dalma --- the Sarkari Five Rupee Lunch House

The five rupee lunch houses created by the pro-people government of Odisha, has remained a non-event for me. They have a few such hunger mitigation joints in Odisha's capital city, Bhubaneswar, which is also a Smart City. Initially I had only an outside view of one such centre that is on my way to the Petrol Pump. At times I have seen a silent, orderly line of people, about a score or half, inching towards an open door of a hall with a motor van parked quietly in front of the feeding-centre. My guess is such a centre would continue till our society became strong enough to sweep it away as an avoidable aberration.

A few years ago, however, I was involuntarily drawn towards the five rupee programme. My housekeeper handed me a piece of paper on which the grocer had written the items and price of goods purchased by him on credit during the month. Besides items like detergent powder, cakes of soap, packets of coriander seeds, Biscuits, Tea, the list contained details about Arhar Dal purchase. On repeated questioning, the boy would not tell me how much the price was of Arhar Dal he had bought that day. Apparently his job was only to carry the goods and the chit.

On scrutiny, I found Two kilograms of Dal had been billed at Rs.324/- on the 7th of October. From earlier records

I found yet another chit which showed 2 kgs of Arhar Dal having been charged Rs 190/- on 24th February and yet another chit showed 2 kgs of Arhar Dal at Rs 230/- on the 7th August. Market being on fire, has by now, stopped giving me burning pain. I keep the chits as coolly as they are presented to me by the housekeeper and at the end of the month, I smilingly write a cheque before the helpful grocer, hand it over to him and let the housekeeper a fresh lease for marauding his shop and my finance. It has been a part of a friendly match being played in life. There is no rancor on losing; no throwing of bottles at the winning players or the pitch. Since government has become indifferent to cursing, I have stopped saying one and defiling my persona. But for another reason, the other day, I felt drawn towards the feeding-centre.

Two persons I know had had their lunch in one of the centres the other day. Both had been to the Hospital to help a sick person and had their food in a centre operating in the campus. Neither had been to such a centre in the past. One of the two is our Driver cum Housekeeper. I listened to him and he answered all my questions. The rice was not raw rice (Arua chawal) he is used to eating. It was par-boiled rice. It was not cooked soft and, therefore, he could not take more than two portions which meant he was used to eating more rice at home when the rice was Arua and was cooked soft.

I was more on Dalma, the Elixir. "Was it made of Arhar Dal?" I asked. He kept mum. I repeated my question. "Maybe, I am not sure", he said. "What were the vegetables used"? I asked. He could not see any, he said. The vegetables had been mixed well in the lentil, he explained. "Did it taste great? I asked. He was not sure. He, however, looked a bit sad.

I thought of the unemployed youths who thronged the smart city and after having food at the feeding-centre would again walk a few miles before returning home, still without a job.

Dalma was no substitute for a job. My government would not realise this. With Arhar Dal costing Rs162/- per kg, Dalma too had already lost its taste.

❑

Rising Debt Burden of Odisha

Some concern has been expressed recently over the rising per capita debt burden due to increasing borrowings of Odisha government. In the current year (2021-22) Government will pay 13.84% of its total expenditure towards repayment of loan and spend Rs 23,521 crore towards this, whereas it will spend just a little higher amount, Rs 25,788 crore (15.17%), on building capital assets, like roads, bridges, irrigation facilities etc. It proposes to incur fresh loan of Rs 40,986 crore that is more than what it would collect through own Taxes—Rs 37,500 crore. The current year will end up with a fiscal deficit of Rs 20,465 crore (3.49 % of the GSDP). Total loan of the Government by the end of the current year would be Rs 1.25 lakh crore as against the projected Gross State Domestic Product (GSDP) of Rs 5.86 lakh crore (21.3%). Total outstanding public debt of the State as on 31st March 2020 stood at Rs.92,775.18 crore, that was 17.8 percent of GSDP.

Total stock of debts, however, is increasing over time and would double between 2016-17 and 2021-22 (Rs 62,135 crore to Rs 1,25,000 crore). Though it is a matter of concern, public debt of Odisha is still sustainable, meaning the Government can service its debts without difficulty. The state is performing within the limits of 25% prescribed under the Fiscal Responsibility and Budget Management (FRBM) Act, 2005 for the Debt to GSDP ratio.

Government feels that future debt outlook of the State is also reasonably comfortable despite difficulties arising out of the pandemic. In the medium term, the total debt to GSDP ratio of the State, Government expects to reach a level of 22.46 per cent in 2023-24. The ratio of total interest payment to total revenue receipts (IPRR) under the FRBM Act is 15%. It is estimated at 6.37% in 2021-22.

Expenditure on Salary, Pension and Interest payment is the major component of revenue expenditure. This has first charge on the resources of the government. It constitutes the major share of the State's total expenditure. Revenue Expenditure also includes expenditure on different programmes of the government which are not of capital nature. In 2018-19, it was Rs 85,356.41 crore and increased to Rs 99,137 crore in 2019-20, Rs 104,864 crore in 2020-21 and estimated to be Rs 119,567 crore this year (21-22). Its share to the total expenditure has been 74.9%, 79.2%, 77.67% and 70.3% respectively. In the current year's Budget of Rs 170,000 crore, capital expenditure related to creation of capital assets is only 13.84% - a mere Rs 23,521 crore.

. The Annual Establishment Review of the state government for 2019-20 revealed that about 2 lakh (1,99,957) government posts remained vacant. There are also thousands of employees who are engaged not on regular scale of pay but on payment of a consolidated amount.

Measures like keeping about two lakh posts vacant and engaging a large number of staff on payment of consolidated amount have been adopted to keep fiscal deficit at a manageable level. This has, however, been at great cost to quality of governance. There are not enough teachers, medical staff and not even enough policemen. Crimes against women and children are numerous and the track-record of the state in the area of controlling crime against women and children is a matter of grave concern. Many critical areas of development remain starved of funds.

During 2015-21, average spending on Education by states has been 15.9% of their Budget. Delhi spent the highest at 26.1%, whereas Odisha spent 15%. In Agriculture and Allied sectors, the average spending was 6.4%, with Chhattisgarh spending the highest at 18.1% against Odisha's 8.1%. In Health sector the average spending was 5.3% and Odisha spent that much while Delhi spent the highest at 12.8%. In Housing and Urban development, Odisha spent much less than the average.

A sound Budget ensures holistic development of the economy through equitable funding of critical sectors. Populist schemes don't strengthen economy; it depletes scarce resources for short term gains. In case of Tamil Nadu, Revenue deficit has been a recurring feature since 2013, and, in 2020-21, it stood at 3.16% of the GSDP while the fiscal deficit was 4.43% of the GSDP. Odisha is Revenue surplus but the fiscal deficit projected at 3.49% of the GSDP is a wakeup call. It calls for curbing profligacy and high degree of financial prudence.

❑

The Raging Drug Menace

A silent storm is sweeping Odisha. Use of drugs and intoxicants has reached menacing proportions. Odisha's alcohol use is higher than country's average. So also, are the use of cannabis, opioid and sedatives.

A report of the Ministry of Social Justice and Empowerment of Government of India on Substance use magnitude of India, 2019 throws light on substance use which means use of illegal drugs or the use of prescription or over-the-counter drugs or alcohol for purposes other than those for which they are meant to be used, or in excessive amounts. Prevalence of current alcohol use indicates that Odisha's alcohol use is higher than country's average. 31.8% of males in the age group of 10-75 years and 16.4% of the population in this age group use alcohol. Odisha was, in 2018, among the top ten states in regard to the number of people in need of help for alcohol problems with as many as 21 lakh people in need of help. 4.9 lakh people (third highest in the country) are in need of help for cannabis related problems; 3 lakh people are in need of help for opioid related problems and 1.2 lakh in need of help in sedative related problems. Odisha ranked third, after Sikkim and Nagaland, on prevalence of use of charas/ganja in the age group of 10-75 years. Among opium, heroin (brown sugar, smack) and pharmaceutical opioids, heroin is most commonly used opioid. In Odisha three lakh people are in need of help for opioid related problems. With 0.8% of its population in the age group of 10-75 years who use opioids in 2018, Odisha's use is higher than the country average. Odisha with 1.2 lakh people in need of help in sedative related problems was 8th in the list of states with such problem. In 2018, 0.31% of its population in age group of 10-75 years used sedatives which were higher than the country average.

India's geographical location - proximity to the major opium producing regions of South West and South East Asia, known as the 'Golden Crescent' and the 'Golden Triangle', respectively - makes it an active region of transit for drugs, either coming from or bound for Europe, Africa, South East Asia or North America. India, as such, has become increasingly vulnerable to transit, trafficking and consumption of opium derivatives in various forms. While a few Metros are major drug consumption spots, many smaller cities are major transit points and consumption spots as well. International Narcotic Control Strategy Report for 2021 refers to significant pharmaceutical drug abuse in the country. Report says, "accurate estimates of the extent, pattern and nature of its drug problem are difficult to quantify. Commonly abused drugs in India include heroin, opium, cocaine, ephedrine, cannabis, and MDMA (ecstasy)."

Experts feel drug supply from Afghanistan will increase with the Taliban takeover. Recently, in India's biggest drug haul, Indian officials reportedly seized nearly three tons of heroin estimated to be worth $2.72 Billion in Gujarat originating from Afghanistan. Some quantities of Drug keep coming regularly to Odisha. Brown sugar worth Rs 40 lakh was seized at Jaleswar on 18th September 2021; three persons including a woman were arrested. Illegal immigrants are suspected to be carriers from neighbouring country. It calls for more effective interception of illegal entry through sea route. On 21st September, 70 grams of brown sugar and a revolver with live cartridges were reportedly seized by police in Bharatpur area of Bhubaneswar. On September 22, Police seized 40 grams of brown sugar at Malatipatpur near Puri, seized vehicles, mobile phones, weighing machine and arrested three persons. A government vehicle is alleged to have been used to bring the brown sugar. Total seizure of brown sugar in Odisha per year was limited within 3 kg per year since 2013. It, however, increased to 34.2 kg in 2020 and in 2021 till end of August, the seized quantity is 34.457 kg.

Odisha has been stepping up enforcement drive with more destruction of Ganja crops, more seizures of ganja, brown sugar, registration of more cases and more arrests under NDPS Act. While Ganja crop was destroyed in 4,632 acres in 2017-18, enforcement authorities destroyed crops in 23,537 acres in the crop year of 2020-21. Seizure of Ganja increased from 371 quintals in 2013 to 1549 quintals in 2020. Cases registered under NDPS Act in 2013 was only 364 cases and 442 persons arrested. The number of cases increased to 1217 in 2020 while the number of arrestees was 1896. In the current year(2021) , about 1249 quintals Ganja have been seized till end of July. About 60% of this has been seized from Koraput, Rayagada, Malkangiri, Kandhamal and Ganjam districts.

In view of the serious dimension the drug menace has assumed in Odisha, there has to be adequate strategy to control the problem. Government needs to address urgently issues like adequate staffing, training, adequate equipment and inter-agency coordination challenges. Enforcement agencies need greater ability to collect and analyse data and conduct complex investigations of criminal drug trafficking.

❑

Growing Squabbles Between Babus and People's Representatives

In the 2019 Election to the Odisha Assembly, 236.66 lakh voters had cast valid votes out of the total registered voters numbering 324.98 lakhs. Nearly 27% --- about 87.09 lakh voters—had abstained from voting. Biju Janata Dal (BJD) polled about 105.72 lakh votes and won 112 seats out of 146 seats contested. About 219.26 lakh voters did not vote for the BJD though BJD secured a landslide victory with a huge majority in the legislature. The result is we in Odisha have the Party that is in power and rules the state, won the Election where for every vote cast in its favour there were two people who did not vote for it. The beauty of Parliamentary Democracy lies in the privilege of those voters who did not vote for the government and yet retained their right to equal treatment by the government. Government officials and the political leaders of the Party in power need to appreciate this fundamental principle. Raj Dharma is basically to adhere to this principle.

After Independence, and, more so, after the state increased its role as a welfare state, interface between elected representatives of the people and officialdom has increased manifold. By and large, this growing interaction has been pleasant and has helped governance. People's representatives were perceived to be closer to people than officials who were considered to be reticent, behind closed doors and not easily accessible to people. In such a situation, the elected representatives acted as a bridge that connected the people with the officials and many field level difficulties of citizens could get redressed. This process, however, was not always a cakewalk experience. In some cases, the entry of people's representatives into the citadel of Babus was not taken kindly; while some Babus remained stiff and tight lipped, some were cold. Government, therefore, put in place a protocol that set the rules of the game. Officials were now duty bound to extend courtesy, be respectful and be prompt in deciding on matters brought to their notice by the people's representatives. This standard operating procedure improved matters. However, instances of occasional deviation kept coming in.

Today the direct reach of government to citizens has increased exponentially. In Odisha, for example, more than fifty lakh people of Odisha today receive monthly allowances of various kinds under different social security schemes, most important being the old age pension scheme. Around sixty lakh women as Members of six lakh Self Help Groups (SHG) have access to concessional credit for undertaking various income generating activities. Over 300 lakh people get one rupee Rice, lakhs of people have got the benefit of pucca houses. Among job card holders, about forty lakh people are active. 96.5 lakh families have been covered under Biju Swasthya Kalyan Yojana. Almost every household in Odisha today is under one or more beneficiary oriented programme of the Government. The sheer size of Beneficiaries today is gargantuan and in such a situation, the probability of unmerited favour to many beneficiaries is great. This being the position, the people who have got into the privileged club of Government munificence either through backdoor or by dubious methods, remain vulnerable to exploitation. Many rural development schemes provide discretion to local officials on where these would be implemented. There is pressure to exclude areas or people the government of the day may not be comfortable with. There is compliance to such pressure where the concerned official is amenable to political manipulation or is of doubtful integrity. Unjust decisions generate anger in the affected party.

The widespread practice of awarding contract for small development works at the grassroots level to party loyalists has been, by now, fine-tuned resulting in severe quality deficit in various development projects, unjust enrichment and widespread disillusionment of worthy entrepreneurs who are left out. A Big Government and numerous Parastatals have plenty of low hanging fruits to offer to loyalists. The pernicious practice of rewarding loyalists of dubious credentials continues, year after year and discontentment keeps swelling. Unfortunately, the impression that is widespread today is field level officials at the cutting edge levels are being carefully selected to act to orders from above. It is also widely believed that a few officials at the state level yield tremendous influence. These developments have created a widespread impression that today officials are more important than people's representatives. This has generated rift between the political representatives and the officials.

In these circumstances it is only natural that the simmering discontent erupts sometimes. There have been a few incidents recently (January,2023) where people's representatives belonging to Opposition have come in confrontation with officials. It is likely that with the next

Election coming closer, such incidents would only increase in days to come.

The remedy is having a politically neutral bureaucracy, keeping the bureaucrats totally out of political activities and taking recourse to transparent and merit-based selection of people to execute public works instead of rewarding loyalists. Such an arrangement can be done only if the extremely popular and powerful Chief Minister intervenes and shows the Bureaucracy its proper place and directs the political functionaries to stop showering favours on loyalists at grassroots level. In the prevailing situation, however, such a course of action looks most unlikely to happen.

❑

Counting my Small Blessings

I won't know why the noble man would always push into my bag enough fresh green chilies to last till I made another visit to him and a small bunch of coriander leaves after I had bought vegetables and had settled my bill. It could be his way of paying respect to me; it could be because he perhaps liked me. It could be a hangover of an old tradition as well. I have never asked him why he did that; but didn't ever object to it either. Rather, I slowly started considering it as my entitlement, but in tranquil moments I regretted being so mean to entertain such an idea. Ultimately, the nice vegetable vendor won, had his way and I slipped into indebtedness in the quicksand of his generosity. This experience however related to two human beings.

The other experience is even more complex and more inexplicable. I always loved to have many plants in my garden. I also loved Sambar; I loved Upma too. I cannot think of Upma and Sambar being cooked without curry leaves. But never did I buy curry leaves from market nor would I ever not have enough of curry leaves in my kitchen. I never planted even one curry plant, nor even our gardener or housekeeper ever did and yet we have three of them, in good shape, in our garden. How then did they appear in our garden? Who else could have planted them and taken care of them if it wasn't the Eternal Gardener who knows what we don't have but should have!!

❑

Our Public Hospitals

India's District and Regional level public Hospitals have always been meeting venues where the near and distant friends and relations gather to see and take care of the sick, thereby adding strain on the inadequate health and sanitation infrastructure of the hospitals. There is always enough manpower available offering / facilitating various modes of care like paramedical help from the relations and acquaintances, willing errand boys who run to nearby pharmacy to get medicines, syringe, needle, bandage etc. Even elders come from distant places for blessing the sick. Friends and relatives keep visiting occasionally if it is a case of prolonged hospitalisation, many of them carry home cooked food, and some caring ones even bring sweets which the sick man was fond of in his/her childhood. This ever-increasing phenomenon even facilitates ancillary commercial activity close to the Beds of the sick. One can see itinerant tea, snacks, fruit vendors and, even sellers of toiletries in the morning hours in various wards. Once I had spotted a newspaper vendor loudly reading out important headlines even inside an important Department of the Cuttack Medical College in late Nineties. Even some new corporate hospitals seem reverential to this practice.

With such an elaborate informal support system

around a patient, the Doctors, on night duty, have little difficulty in having some sleep-in peace. In this situation, the Survivor, on reaching home, gets a hero's welcome and, the Dead, the respect of a fallen fighter.

❑

The Deity on the Dark Lane

On the dimly lit lane with wide canopied Gulmohar trees on both sides, she looked no more than a speck while I had my walk early in the morning. She sat on dust, on the edge of the road and diffidently stretched her frail right hand when someone would pass her way. I have no idea if she ever made a voice request. Even if she did, it could have been in whispers, very low in decibel strength. With extremely low body mass index, her voice couldn't have been more demanding than a quivering whisper. With all mundane factors for a healthy living denied to her, she strangely stood out as something extraordinary. She exuded tremendous amount of compassion almost to the point of saturating the surroundings and added great value to the lonely lane. She, I always felt, was the presiding deity who blessed all the passersby. A few made offerings, most didn't. Her persona remained contented both with and without a coin. The other day a group of young morning walkers, who walked faster, overtook me. I noticed one of them stopping at her and giving a coin. He kept standing, with both hands folded. It seemed a long prayer, like one said when one was in great distress. He moved only when I got closer. I am no privy to his woes; but whatever those were; those could not have been in more competent hands for getting relief.

❑

My Friend

He was not a celebrity that people would accost him on the street and ask for an autograph; but this morning when I saw him from a distance, I did go off my beaten track to greet him precisely because he was dear to me. For about a month I was looking forward to seeing him on the lane, having his slow walk.

He had always looked to me a private person, happy, contented, reticent, unassuming, away from ambition, arrogance and flamboyancy. Once I had suggested that he should do some business on his own if he was disinclined to work in any organisation under a boss. He said he was too old for starting something new. He was now waiting for his son to start working soon after he completed his study in two years. He seemed to be in love with his anonymity. While walking, burning calories was never in his agenda. He walked slowly; he covered short distance.

His way of greeting me on road was special. He made efforts to raise his heavy hands and took some time to bring both flabby palms together. Raising both the palms in unison to Namaskar posture was quite an effort. But he underwent this difficult exercise most enthusiastically when I saw me.

Seeing me approaching him, his round face put on the usual benign smile. I felt reassured when he said he was not unwell. "It was the rain," he said, that had kept him away from walk. I looked into his eyes again, to read his thoughts and feel if he was not keeping anything from me. He smiled back, looking straight into my eyes. I believed his smile.

The world around that had looked somewhat indisposed in his absence, suddenly turned cheerful and healthy.

❑

GLOSSARY

1.	Avatar	------	Incarnation
2.	Aam Admi	------	Common man
3.	Ahimsa	------	Nonviolence
4.	Arhar	------	Pigeon pea
5.	Anantasayanam	------	Cosmic Hibernation-- silent sleeping nature of universe
6.	Ashram	------	Hermitage
7.	Barnamala	------	Alphabet
8.	Bajra	------	A type of millet
9.	Bara	------	Indian snack made from ground lentils that is deep fried
10.	Baidya	------	Practitioner of Ayurvedic medicine
11.	Bidyapitha	------	School
12.	Bhaat	------	Rice
13.	Chaiwala	------	Tea seller
14.	Chhapan Bhog	------	Fifty six varieties of cooked offerings to God
15.	Chironji	------	A dry fruit, a nutty seed from the plant Buchanania lanzan
16.	Chulah	------	Fireplace, Stove
17.	Dal	------	Pulse, a dish made with lentils
18.	Dalma	------	Lentil cooked with vegetables
19.	Devi	------	Goddess
20.	Ganja	------	Cannabis
21.	Indrajava	------	A flowering plant species with medicinal properties
22.	Jowar	------	A type of millet, sorghum
23.	Kutir Jyoti	------	Cottage electrification
24.	Lakh	------	A hundred thousand
25.	Mandia	------	Finger millet
26.	Maggi	------	Popular brand of a snack of ready to cook spiced noodle
27.	Mahaprasad	------	Food offered to Lord Jagannath in Puri
28.	Matha	------	Religious monastery
29.	Mohua	------	A tropical tree with edible flowers and oil seeds
30.	Neti	------	Nasal cleansing through irrigation.
31.	Pahari	------	Pertaining to hilly region
32.	Pakoda	------	Spicy snack consisting of meat or vegetables fried in batter
33.	Pakhala	------	Cooked rice, a little fermented in water
34.	Pohala	------	A variety of fish – Reba carp
35.	Phagu Purnima	------	Full moon day of the eleventh month of Hindu calender
36.	Pitha	------	Pancake
37.	Sarkari	------	Relating to Government
38.	Sabitri Brata	------	A fasting day observed by married ladies on no moon day in month of Jyeshtha
39.	Swamiji	------	Hindu title of respect, especially for a Hindu religious teacher
40.	Samosa	------	A fried pastry with filling of spiced potatoes and peas
41.	Surya Namaskar	------	Sun salutation in sequence of 12 yoga postures
42.	Vana Sanrakshana Samitis	------	Groups for protection of forests

Black Eagle Books

www.blackeaglebooks.org
info@blackeaglebooks.org

Black Eagle Books, an independent publisher, was founded
as a nonprofit organization in April, 2019. It is our mission
to connect and engage the Indian diaspora and the world at
large with the best of works of world literature published
on a collaborative platform, with special emphasis on
foregrounding Contemporary Classics and New Writing.

www.ingramcontent.com/pod-product-compliance
Lightning Source LLC
Chambersburg PA
CBHW020539030426
42337CB00013B/908